OPENING THE HEART OF THE COSMOS

Opening the Heart of the Cosmos

Insights on the Lotus Sutra

Thich Nhat Hanh

PARALLAX PRESS
BERKELEY, CA

Parallax Press
P.O. Box 7355
Berkeley, CA 94707
www.parallax.org

Parallax Press is the publishing division of Unified Buddhist Church, Inc.

Cover art by Dong Nguyen
Cover and text design by Gopa & Ted 2, Inc.

Library of Congress Cataloging-in-Publication Data

Nhât Hanh, Thích.
  Opening the heart of the cosmos : insights on the Lotus Sutra / Thích Nhât Hanh.
    p. cm.
  ISBN 1-888375-33-7 (hardcover)
   1. Tripitaka. Sūtrapitaka. Saddharmapundarīkasūtra—Criticism, interpretation, etc. I.
Title.
  BQ2057 .N53 2003
  294.3'85—dc22

1 2 3 4 5 / 07 06 05 04 03

❧ *Contents*

At night as I recite the *Lotus Sutra*
The sound moves the galaxies
The earth below wakes up
In her lap suddenly flowers appear

At night as I recite the *Lotus Sutra*
A jeweled stupa appears resplendent
All over the sky bodhisattvas are seen
And Buddha's hand is in mine.

—Thich Nhat Hanh

❧ Introduction

THE *Lotus Sutra* is known as the "King of Sutras." The Sanskrit title, *Saddharmapundarika-sutra*, means "The Lotus
Blossom of the Wonderful Dharma." For many centuries Buddhist
practitioners have revered it as the most beautiful flower in the garden
of the Mahayana Buddhist sutras.

While there are a few English translations of the *Lotus Sutra* available, in general its particular message of inclusiveness and reconciliation has not been well known in the West.[1] This book shows how the
teachings of the sutra can help us realize the practices of mindfulness,
compassion, and love for the well-being of our family, our community, our society, and the world.

The Historical and the Ultimate Dimensions

Like many Mahayana texts, the *Lotus Sutra* was composed and compiled in stages over several centuries.[2] We think of the Buddha delivering the *Lotus Sutra* on the Gridhrakuta Mountain (Vulture Peak) in
India sometime toward the end of his lifetime (c. 485–565 B.C.E). We
also know from modern textual study and research that the sutra was
compiled, written down, and circulated about 700 years later, at the
end of the second century.[3]

The twenty-eight chapters of the *Lotus Sutra* have generally been
divided into two parts.[4] The first part focuses on the historical dimension, which is concerned with what happened in Shakyamuni's lifetime. This is the historical Buddha seen through our ordinary way of
perception. In the historical dimension, we can see that a person
named Siddhartha Gautama was born, grew up, left home to seek spiritual truth, practiced and attained a great realization, and became the
Buddha. He shared his realization and taught the Dharma for the rest

of his eighty years of earthly life and then passed into nirvana. Vulture Peak is a real place in India, and you can still go and visit the site where Shakyamuni delivered many of his greatest teachings.

The second part deals with the ultimate dimension. The ultimate dimension shows us the existence of the Buddha on a different plane, a plane that goes beyond our ordinary perception of space and time. This is the Buddha as a living reality, the Buddha as the Dharma body (*dharmakaya*). In the ultimate dimension, we are not concerned with ideas such as birth and death, coming and going, subject and object. The ultimate dimension is true reality, nirvana, the Dharma realm (*dharmadhatu*) beyond all such dualisms.

In order to deliver its profound message—that everyone has the capacity for Buddhahood—the *Lotus Sutra* had to show us the ultimate dimension. If we recognize only the historical Buddha Shakyamuni, who taught great disciples like Shariputra and Maudgalyayana while he was alive and predicted their attainment of Buddhahood, we may feel that since we were not fortunate to live in the time of Shakyamuni, there is no one to testify to our potential Buddhahood here and now. This is why the sutra shows us the ultimate dimension of the Buddha, unbound by our conventional understanding of time and space. We do not have to go back 2,500 years in order to hear the message that we too can become a Buddha. We need only to listen very carefully to the message of the sutra and recognize the Buddha of the ultimate dimension.

We need to be able to recognize both the historical and ultimate dimensions in order to open the door of the *Lotus Sutra* so that we can get in touch with the wonderful Dharma. The historical dimension connects us to the Buddha who lived and taught in fifth-century India. This is the human Buddha, whose search for truth and whose practice and path we can emulate. The ultimate dimension reveals the eternal meaning of the Buddha's teachings, the essence of the Dharma that is beyond time and space. As we will discover, we don't have to go somewhere else in order to touch the ultimate dimension. We can touch the joy and freedom of the ultimate dimension right in our everyday life in the historical dimension, just as the Buddha did under the bodhi tree.

While studying the *Lotus Sutra*, we can determine in which dimension the sutra is operating. Whenever everyone's eyes are fixed on the

earth—looking at the trees, plants, hills, mountains, or each other—
then we know we are in the historical dimension, the world of birth and
death. But when everyone's eyes look into space then we have entered
the ultimate dimension, the unborn and undying world.

The sutra shifts between the historical and ultimate in separate chapters and in different scenes within one chapter. If we can recognize
when we are in the historical dimension and when we are in the ultimate dimension, we will not become bewildered or perplexed by the
words of the sutra, especially those used to describe the ultimate dimension. To convey the immeasurable, infinite vastness of this cosmic
dimension, the sutra uses concepts of inexhaustible time and of limitless space, unlike anything we can grasp with our ordinary perception.

Understanding the Meaning of the Words of the Sutra

The language of the *Lotus Sutra* is like a very skillful painting that
appears to be quite real. In order to demonstrate the meaning of the
sutras, vivid language and images are used to point to very deep and
wonderful ideas. The creators of the sutras were very great poets, but
we should remember that such language is only a skillful means to
express the profound ideas of the teachings. So when we read the sutra
we must be able to look deeply. If we are caught up in the words, we
will only see descriptions of miraculous events and supernatural powers and we will not be able to receive the true meaning that the *Lotus
Sutra* wants to teach us.

For example, in Chapter Twenty-One of the *Lotus Sutra*, "The
Supernatural Powers of the Thus Come One," the Buddha performs
a great miracle. He puts out his tongue and covers the trichiliocosm,
a realm of cosmic space too vast for us even to imagine. (This image
comes from an ancient Indian saying that someone who speaks the
truth "speaks with a very large tongue.") And from each of pore of his
skin he sends out innumerable rays of light of all colors that reveal all
the worlds of the ten directions. In Buddhist texts, light symbolizes
enlightenment, and the phrase "ten directions" means the entire cosmos.[5] The intent of this passage is to express the tremendous capacity of the light of mindfulness of someone who is fully awakened. It is

an artful, poetic way of presenting the truth that the light of mindfulness is very strong.

Similarly, Chapter Fifteen of the *Lotus Sutra*, "Welling Up Out of the Earth," describes millions of bodhisattvas with bodies as beautiful as pure gold who spring up from within the earth. They emit wonderful sounds to praise the Buddha and this praise is said to go on for as long as 50 billion *kalpas*. A kalpa is a vast unit of time, an eon. This is really a way of talking about the infinite, limitless nature of time in the ultimate dimension. One second contains thousands of lifetimes and eternity is just one second. The one contains the all.

When we encounter such passages, we should not become caught up in the mystical language. The dramatic language and images are the literary equivalent of a statue of a Buddha seated on a lotus throne, reminding us of the Buddha's capacity to sit mindfully and peacefully.

Opening the Heart of the Cosmos

In Parts One and Two of this book, we look into the historical dimension and the ultimate dimension revealed in the *Lotus Sutra*. The themes presented here can help us put the sutra's teachings of compassion and reconciliation into practice in a beneficial way. This is the path of engaged Buddhism. Our practice and insight can help bring joy, peace, and freedom not only on an individual level but also to our families, our communities, and our planet.

The *Lotus Sutra* affirms that we all have the capacity to become a Buddha. This is a very great gift. How can we best use this wonderful gift we have received? By becoming the arms of the Buddha through our practice in our daily life, in Sangha-building, and in our work in the world. This is why I propose that we develop a third division of the *Lotus Sutra*, the dimension of action, to complement and complete the teachings of the historical and the ultimate dimensions. Parts Three and Four of this book shows us how the *Lotus Sutra* opens the gateway to enter the dimension of action of the bodhisattvas.

In our practice, we have the support of the many great bodhisattvas introduced in this sutra—including Medicine King, Never Disparaging, Earth-Holder, Samantabhadra (the bodhisattva of Great Action),

Avalokiteshvara (the bodhisattva of Great Compassion), and countless other bodhisattvas who live with us in the world. Through our practice and our Sangha insight, we are able to become the hands and arms of the Buddha and carry out the work of healing, transformation, and reconciliation in the world.

The Wide Embrace of the Lotus Sutra

From One Buddhism to Many

ONE REASON the *Lotus Sutra* is called the "King of Sutras" is because it has the capacity to fit together and accept all the schools of Buddhism.

Buddhism is a living reality, and living things are always growing. A tree continually grows more branches, more leaves, and more flowers. In order for Buddhism to stay alive we have to allow it to develop. As we can see in our own time, life is not static. Political, social, economic, cultural, and environmental situations change—often very dramatically and sometimes very quickly. India in the fifth to first centuries B.C.E was no different—in fact this was a time of great religious, cultural, and political change. The Buddha's realization, his ministry and teaching, were themselves a radical departure from the prevailing religious and social structure of India, and many other new religions, such as Jainism, also sprang up at this time.[1] So we can see that the seeds of change and adaptation were in Buddhism from the beginning, and its ability to transform and respond to new ways of life and new kinds of problems is the key to its continuing as a living tradition for over 2,500 years.

Original Buddhism (also called Source Buddhism) comprises the teachings given during the lifetime of the historical Buddha, Shakyamuni. This was the first Buddhism.[2] Original Buddhism was a time of unified Buddhism; there was just one Sutra Collection and one Vinaya Collection. Then came Schools Buddhism, which developed about 150 years after the Buddha's lifetime, when the early Buddhist Sangha split into two schools—the Theravada ("Way of the Elders"), which was conservative in nature; and the Mahasanghikavada ("The Way of the

Majority"), which was more progressive.[3] As time went on, these two schools further divided. The records speak of eighteen schools but we know that at one time there were more, as many as twenty-five or twenty-six schools, each with its own Sutra and Vinaya collection.[4]

The Mahayana way of study and practice arose from the Mahasangika (Majority) school. When that study and practice were sufficiently ripe, the sutras of the Mahayana began to appear. Thus we could say that the formation of Buddhism took place in three stages: 1) Original Buddhism 2) Schools' Buddhism 3) Mahayana Buddhism. The first Mahayana sutras to appear were the Prajnaparamita.

When Mahayana Buddhism began to develop, Mahayana practitioners called the schools which did not belong to Mahayana (Great Vehicle), "Hinayana" (Little Vehicle). The word "little" here decries that kind of Buddhism, saying: Your vehicle cannot carry many people. At the most it can only carry you yourself. Our vehicle on the other hand, is great. It can carry tens, even hundreds of people. The very use of the words "Great" and "Little" shows that there was a sense of competition and self-importance in the Mahayana followers.

As the Buddhist monastic institution developed, the conservative tradition became rather inflexible and insular. Rather than seeking ways of teaching and practice that would be useful in everyday life, the monastic Sangha had a tendency to devote itself to analyzing points of abstract philosophical doctrine, focusing on study of the Abhidharma, the commentary collection. These are additional works written to systematize and further expound the teachings of Buddhism.[5] A hair could be split many times, and the prose of the Abhidharma is full of minutely split hairs. Analysis followed upon analysis and the monk-scholars began to enjoy analysis for analysis's sake. In this environment, the practice of mindfulness was there but it could be rather sterile and mechanical, not leading to peace, joy, happiness, and freedom right in the present moment. The method of interpreting, understanding, and practicing the teachings became quite rigid with a hard-line attitude that was difficult for others to accept.

Locked into this conservative attitude, the monastic Sangha could not fulfill the whole of its responsibility to society. A few hundred years after the Buddha's nirvana, the monastic Sangha was not really engaged, it did not take into account the difficulties of society outside the monastery. Buddhism had to change and grow in order to continue as a living tradition. So around the first century B.C.E a progressive school began to evolve out of the Mahasanghika lineage—the Mahayana. This was a reform movement within Buddhism, a revolutionary movement that reached out to include both monastic and lay followers, a great vehicle that was capable of carrying all living beings to liberation.

The highest spiritual ideal of the Hinayana is the arhat ("worthy one") who through his own effort and practice attains liberation. The monastic sangha was focused only on personal salvation, thinking about nirvana only in individual terms. The Mahayana put forth the ideal of the bodhisattva (*bodhi*, "wisdom, enlightenment," *sattva*, "being"), who shares the fruits of his or her practice with all other beings. The bodhisattva is someone who, upon attaining enlightenment, vows to forgo entering nirvana until all other sentient beings—down to the very last blade of grass—are also liberated. This insight was very profound. Buddhism expressed in Mahayana terms is engaged, quite positive, and very beautiful.

The Mahayana began with this insight and further developed it, and when the study and practice were sufficiently ripe, scriptural texts began to appear, beginning with the Prajnaparamita ("Perfection of Wisdom") sutras, which explored in great depth the principle of non-duality and the understanding of emptiness (*shunyata*). The concept of "emptiness" here is not a form of nihilism as some early Western scholars of Buddhism thought; it simply means that all things are empty of an inherent, unchanging, and permanent nature—no thing exists independently and remains fixed, but arises due to a set of constantly changing causes and conditions. This is the insight of interbeing.

We can see that this insight in the Prajnaparamita sutras arose from such essential Buddhist teachings as dependent co-arising (*pratityasamutpada*).[6] It's important to remember that the Mahayana draws upon the same teachings that are the basis for the Theravada school. Rather than stopping there, however, Mahayana thinkers continued to expand upon these teachings, adding new insights and interpretations to respond to the changing conditions and spiritual needs of the people.

So we should not think of the Mahayana as a rejection of the early Buddhist canon but rather as a continuation and expansion of its insights.

Next to appear was the *Ratnakutna Sutra (Sutra of the Collection of Jewels)*, followed by the *Avatamsaka Sutra (Garland Sutra)*, and culminating in the *Vimalakirtinirdesha Sutra (Discourse of Vimalakirti)*, which describes the accomplishment of a great lay practitioner, Vimalakirti. As described in this sutra, the insight and wisdom of the layman Vimalakirti surpassed the insight and wisdom of all the monastics. Even the spiritual attainment of the Buddha's greatest disciples, such as Shariputra, Purna, and Mahakashyapa, was nothing compared with that of Vimalakirti.

Though the *Vimalakirtinirdesha* has many deep and wonderful teachings, it is not my favorite sutra because it goes a little too far in its reaction to the conservatives and its treatment of the Buddha's original disciples, in particular Shariputra, the most senior of the Buddha's disciples. In the sutra, he is presented as being rather infantile, credulous, and foolish, in contrast to Vimalakirti, who is depicted as very intelligent, a truly great practitioner. But when we study the matter carefully and see the extent of the conservative attitude and rigidity of the monastic sangha, we can better understand why this and other Mahayana texts took such a critical stance.

These Mahayana sutras—the *Vimalakirtinirdesha* in particular—were a kind of heavy artillery firing into the monastic institution, which no longer provided the kind of spiritual guidance that people needed to put the teachings into practice in their daily lives. On the other hand, the *Lotus Sutra*, was the first Mahayana sutra to use loving speech and the first to accept all schools and tendencies of Buddhism. Therefore the *Lotus Sutra* is like a cool breeze, a gentle rain, assuaging the stifling atmosphere of contention between the conservatives and the progressives.

The Theravada school taught that there was only one bodhisattva, the past lives of the historical person Siddhartha Gautama, who became the Buddha. According to the Hinayana, the best some us could do was to become an arhat, and that only after many lifetimes of practice. Unable to dedicate themselves to the kind of austere practices required of monastics, lay Buddhists began to focus only on providing support to the monastic sangha in order to gain merit that would help them to a favorable rebirth. People did not believe they could become a Buddha so they didn't feel the need to practice in order to become a Buddha.

The Mahayana thinkers saw the great danger of this. Among the early Mahayana philosophers were many intelligent laypeople as well as a number of monastics who saw that there was a risk that Buddhism would die as a living tradition if the monastic sangha did not open up to the world. Noting that the Buddha mentions the existence of other Buddhas in early sutras, they concluded that if there are many Buddhas there must also be many bodhisattvas. In the Mahayana sutras, Shariputra is predicted to attain Buddhahood. The significance of this is that every disciple of the Buddha, the original sangha of the *shravakas* ("word-hearers," those who directly heard the Buddha's teaching), also has the capacity to become a Buddha. What was possible for Siddhartha, and for Shariputra and the other shravakas, is also possible for each of us.

This is the great insight of the Mahayana—that *everyone* can become a Buddha. What Siddhartha achieved, all of us can also achieve, whether we are a man or a woman, no matter what social class or ethnic group we were born into, or whether we practice as a monastic or as a layperson. We all have the capacity to become a fully enlightened Buddha. And while on the path to becoming a fully enlightened Buddha, we are all bodhisattvas.

The new development of the Mahayana rejuvenated Buddhism and there was a lot of enthusiasm in the air. But the Mahayana as a well-defined community was not yet a reality. At that time the bodhisattva precepts had not yet been developed. The monastic sangha had the Five Mindfulness Trainings and the *Pratimoksha* to rely on, but the guidelines for the practice of the bodhisattva had not yet been created.[7] Then, in the *Brahmajala Sutra* (*Sutra of the Net of Brahma*), the bodhisattva pratimoksha was set out—fifty-eight precepts to be shared and practiced by both lay and monastic bodhisattvas. The Fourteen Mindfulness Trainings of the Order of Interbeing are a modern version of these bodhisattva precepts. They are of exactly the same nature and are shared by both monastic and lay practitioners.[8]

Mahayana Buddhists also saw the need to begin forming sanghas of both monastic and lay practitioners. There are many sutras reflecting this period of time when sangha-building was taken up by monastics (monks, *bhikshus*, and nuns, *bhikshunis*) together with male and female lay practitioners (*upasakas* and *upasikas*). The *Lotus Sutra* appeared during this crucial period in the development of the Mahayana, and it represented a beautiful reconciliation between the early tradition of the shravakas and the bodhisattva path, the expansive, inclusive vehicle of the Mahayana. The two traditions were unified as the One Vehicle that can carry all beings to the shore of liberation.

The Role of the Lotus Sutra

Right from the beginning, in the Prajnaparamita sutras and culminating in the *Vimalakirtinirdesha*, we see extreme expressions of thought and language in the Mahayana scriptures. They were skillful, sometimes quite harsh, polemics aimed at breaking the stranglehold of the traditional congregation. The ideas expressed in these sutras are very deep and wonderful, but they do not show the gentle countenance of the true, mature Mahayana.

Before the appearance of the *Lotus Sutra*, many profound Mahayana ideas and philosophies had already been developed, and had begun to be admired by many people. But the Mahayana was only there as a number of individuals scattered here and there. It was an expression of thought and scripture, but it was not yet there in the form of a community, an organization, or an establishment. Only when the *Lotus Sutra* was born, with its spirit of moderation, reconciliation, and unity, did the Mahayana begin to have a complete sangha of monks, nuns, and laypeople. This is the environment in which the *Lotus Sutra* was born, and its appearance was a very fortunate occurrence that contributed to the foundation of Mahayana Buddhism at just the right time. The *Lotus Sutra* applied a new method that was very compassionate and inclusive in order to reconcile the traditional shravaka path with the new *bodhisattvayana*, the path of the bodhisattva.

The attitude of reconciliation and harmony reflected in the *Lotus*

Sutra was very important in the maturation of Mahayana Buddhism. Because of the sutra's capacity to accept and integrate the paths of all the Buddhist vehicles, it has been given the highest place in the Mahayana canon. In the *Lotus Sutra* the Buddha says to Bodhisattva Beflowered by the King of Constellation, "Just as among all streams, rivers, and bodies of water the sea is the first, the Sutra of the Dharma Blossom is the deepest and greatest among the scriptures preached by the Thus Come One."[9] And earlier in the sutra, the Buddha says:

> *Medicine King, I now proclaim to you*
> *The scriptures that I preach;*
> *And among these scriptures*
> *The Dharma Blossom is foremost.*[10]

The Literary Style of the Lotus Sutra

When we read the Mahayana sutras, it may seem that the verse sections are there to summarize the prose sections. When I was young, I thought the sutras had a verse section because poetry is easier to remember by heart than prose. When the *Lotus Sutra* first arose, sutras were generally written in verse form and not in prose. It's rather like the store of proverbial folksong in Vietnam or the Greek epics of Homer which originally were also transmitted orally. The sutras of the Mahayana were the same. In the beginning, the sutras appeared in the form of verses which were passed on orally. So it is in verse form that the *Lotus Sutra* first made its appearance and the prose sections were added later, to expand upon and further explain the teachings in verse.

The reason for this is for the first 400 years during and after the Buddha's lifetime, his teachings were transmitted orally, memorized and recited by the shravakas. In order to be easier to understand and learn by heart, the teachings were transmitted in verse form in a poetic language called Prakrit. This language had its own metric rules rather like we might find in English poetry, for instance in the poem "The Fountain" by Wordsworth, one line is eight syllables and the next line is six syllables:

> *We talked with open heart and tongue*
> *affectionate and true.*
> *A pair of friends though I was young,*
> *and Matthew seventy-two.*[11]

It's very easy to remember and understand. Nevertheless, because this literary style has its own particular form and metrical rules it is difficult to change it or to translate it into a different language. In the second stage of the appearance of the *Lotus Sutra* people added the prose part with the aim of making the verse parts clearer in meaning. For instance, when Wordsworth writes about a tongue which was *affectionate and true* it doesn't just mean that the tongue is affectionate and true, it means that the two people are affectionate and true to each other. The prose is able to speak more extensively and use more words to explain the verse portions.

So the earliest form of Buddhist teachings were in verse, and only later, when the teachings began to be recorded in written form in Sanskrit, the classical language of religion and philosophy of India, did long prose sections, called *sutra*, emerge. The word "sutra" means "thread" in Sanskrit, so a sutra is a thread of prose that links and expands upon the verse form of a teaching.

As we read the *Lotus Sutra* and other Mahayana sutras, it is important to remember this because these texts were not just recorded once and for all in one form. The *Lotus Sutra* went through four periods of development, beginning with its original form of spoken verses. In the second stage, the verses were recorded in written form. In the third stage, more prose sections were added. When we compare the Sanskrit versions with each other we see that there are versions whose prose part is shorter than that of others.[12] This means that the *Lotus Sutra* grew up like a large tree, sending out new sprouts, new shoots and new branches as time went on. In the mid-second century it was still quite a small tree. But by the end of the second century it had grown a great deal.

In the fourth stage, the Sutra was given new chapters. In the Chinese version of Kumarajiva, the *Lotus Sutra* has twenty-eight chapters and in the Sanskrit version which we presently have it has twenty-seven.[13] Recent research has shown that from chapter twenty-three onwards new chapters have been added. Maybe when people were using the *Lotus Sutra*, they saw its shortcomings and so they added new chapters later on. In order to make them seem like original parts of the *Lotus Sutra*, verse sections were added back in afterward.[14]

At that time in India scholarship prospered, and many new theories and currents of thought arose. Philosophical and literary works of the time were all written in Sanskrit. Buddhist literature also had to take on new forms. A number of scholars adapted the *Lotus Sutra* from Prakrit, the language of the people, into Sanskrit, the language generally used by scholars and in literature It is rather like the time when the French had just come to Vietnam. The Chinese and native Vietnamese languages were suppressed and people who were able to speak French were seen to be civilized and respected.

Prakrit and Sanskrit are related to each other, but their syntax and semantics are very different and while it was not difficult to adapt the prose section from Prakrit to Sanskrit, it was very difficult to translate the verse sections. Therefore the Sanskrit in the *Lotus Sutra*, as in a number of other sutras, is Buddhist Hybrid Sanskrit, a language which is a mixture of Sanskrit and Prakrit. If you were to read a section of the *Lotus Sutra* in the Chinese version translated from Sanskrit by the Venerable Kumarajiva, it reads much more smoothly.

Something else to remember when reading the *Lotus Sutra* is its theatricality. At the time of the development of the Mahayana, India was undergoing a period of cultural renewal and famous religious and literary epics such as the *Ramayana* and the *Mahabharata* were made into theatrical presentations.[15] This is the way many people in rural India received an education in religious and cultural traditions. The Buddhists presented the sutras as drama, with each chapter like an act in a play. Many teachings are illustrated in parables, and the characters of the shravakas, bodhisattvas, and Buddhas are depicted very colorfully. The action is presented in wondrous settings, like stage sets, that are described in vivid detail. This way of presenting the teachings can appeal to people of different social classes, educational levels, and so on. So the dramatic structure of the sutras makes them accessible to more people.

The *Lotus Sutra* is not a scholarly work for specialists. It is more of a popular work with universal appeal which can be applied in practice. As we read the *Lotus Sutra*, we see how it has inherited the essence and the ideas of the Mahayana sutras which preceded it. For example, it has inherited the teachings of emptiness from the *Prajnaparamita* sutras, the teachings of the multiple layers of causation from the *Avatamsaka* Sutra and the idea of the liberation which goes beyond all conceptualisation from the *Vimalakirtinirdesha*. However, the way the *Lotus Sutra* presents these ideas is not academic. The *Lotus Sutra* takes Buddhism forward an enormous step because of it universal appeal and practical nature. The strength of the *Lotus Sutra* lies in its ability to present abstruse teachings simply in a way which is easy to understand and applicable to all walks of life.

❧ Part I

The Historical Dimension

The Two Doors

CHAPTER ONE of the *Lotus Sutra*, "Introduction," takes us to Vulture Peak, near the city of Rajagriha in the kingdom of Magadha (present-day northeast India), where the Buddha has gathered with a large assembly of disciples including Kashyapa, Shariputra, Maudgalyayana, and Ananda, as well thousands of bhikshus and bhikshunis, including the Buddha's aunt, Mahaprajapati and his former wife, Yashodhara. In addition, there are tens of thousands of great bodhisattvas in attendance, among them Manjushri, Avalokiteshvara, Medicine King (Bhaisajyaraja), and Maitreya. Also present are many thousands of gods, including Indra, and the kings of the *nagas, kinnaras, ghandharvas, asuras,* and *garudas*.[1] The ruler of Magadha, King Ajatashatru, and his royal family and retinue, are also in attendance. This vast multitude of many different kinds of beings was present in the assembly when the Buddha was about to deliver the *Lotus Sutra.*

This chapter not only sets the stage for the delivery of the sutra in the historical dimension but also reveals the ultimate dimension. It thus serves as a general introduction to the entire text. Just as in a theatrical presentation, it introduces the characters of the play we are about to see. The vast numbers of shravakas and bodhisattvas, the presence of gods and mythical beings, give us our first taste of the ultimate dimension and show us that the opportunity to hear the *Lotus Sutra* delivered by the Buddha is something very special, a great occurrence not to be missed.

First, the Buddha delivered a Mahayana sutra called the *Sutra of Immeasurable Meaning,* then entered a state of meditative concentration (*samadhi*). While he was in this concentration, heavenly flowers rained from the sky and the earth quaked. Then the Buddha sent out a ray of light from his *ushnisha*, illuminating various cosmic realms.[2] The entire assembly was able to see these worlds appear very clearly, and everyone was most surprised and delighted at the wonderful event that was taking place around them. In all these worlds, Buddhas could be seen giving Dharma talks to great assemblies of bhikshus, bhikshunis, upasakas, and upasikas—exactly like the Buddha's disciples in this world.

When this wonderful event took place, Bodhisattva Maitreya, who is also called Ajita ("Unconquered One"), said to himself, "Today the World-Honored One is going to do something very special, that is why he sent out this ray of light and performed this miracle." He turned to Bodhisattva Manjushri and asked him, "Why has the Buddha manifested these unusual signs?" And Manjushri replied, "Today the World-Honored One wishes to give a great teaching, to cause the rain of the Dharma to fall, to beat the great drum of the Dharma." He described a similar occurrence he had witnessed, when a Buddha called Sun and Moon Glow (Chandrasuryapradipa) had also delivered the *Sutra on the Immeasurable Meaning*, entered samadhi, caused flowers to rain from the sky, and emitted a ray of light that illuminated all the cosmic realms. Then that Buddha had taught the *Lotus Sutra*. So Manjushri said, "Today the World-Honored One, our teacher Shakyamuni, will also teach the *Lotus Sutra*."

The intention of this introductory chapter is to prepare the audience psychologically and spiritually to receive a very important teaching, the Scripture of the Lotus Blossom of the Wonderful Dharma. In order to understand the great import of this teaching, the assembly that has gathered in this historical dimension must be introduced to the ultimate dimension. In the past, in another cosmic realm, the Buddha Sun and Moon Glow had also given the teaching of the *Lotus Sutra*. So the miraculous events that are happening today are only a repetition of something that has already occurred in another dimension of reality, the ultimate dimension that is unbounded by our ordinary perceptions of time and space.

As far as the historical dimension is concerned, Shakyamuni is the Buddha who is giving the Dharma talk today in this *Saha* world.[3] From this perspective, the Buddha gave teachings for forty years, and then only at the end of his life did he give the teaching of the *Lotus Sutra.* But in terms of the ultimate dimension, Buddha Shakyamuni and Buddha Sun and Moon Glow are one and the same. In the ultimate dimension, never for a moment has the Buddha ceased to deliver the *Lotus Sutra.*

So this introductory chapter opens two doors. The first door is that of history, the events we experience and what we can see and know in our own lifetimes. The second door is that of ultimate reality, which goes beyond time and space. Everything—all phenomena—participates in these two dimensions. When we look at a wave on the surface of the ocean, we can see the form of the wave and we locate the wave in space and time. Looking at a wave from the perspective of the historical dimension, it seems to have a beginning and an end, a birth and a death. A wave can be high or low, a wave can be long or short—many qualities can be ascribed to the wave. The notions of "birth" and "death," "high" or "low," "beginning" and "ending," "coming" and "going," "being" or "nonbeing"—all of these can be applied to a wave in the historical dimension.

We, too, are subject to these notions. When we look from the historical dimension we see that we are subject to being and nonbeing. We are born but later on we will die. We have a beginning and an end. We have come from somewhere and we will go somewhere. That is the historical dimension. All of us belong to this dimension. Shakyamuni Buddha also has a historical dimension—he was a human being who was born in Kapilavastu and died in Kushinagara, and during his lifetime of eighty years he taught the Dharma.

At the same time, all beings and things also belong to the ultimate dimension, the dimension of reality that is not subject to notions of space and time, birth and death, coming and going. A wave is a wave but at the same time it is water. The wave does not have to die in order to become water; it is already water right in the present moment. We don't speak of water in terms of being or nonbeing, coming and going—water is always water. To talk about a wave, we need these notions: the wave arises and passes away; it comes from somewhere or has gone somewhere; the wave has a beginning and an end; it is high or low, more or less beautiful than other waves; the wave is subject to birth and death. None of these distinctions can be applied to the wave in its ultimate dimension as water. In fact, you cannot separate the wave from its ultimate dimension.

Even though we are used to seeing everything in terms of the historical dimension, we can touch the ultimate dimension. So our practice is to become like a wave—while living the life of a wave in the historical dimension, we realize that we are also water and live the life of water. That is the essence of the practice. Because if you know your true nature of no coming, no going; no being, no nonbeing; no birth, no death, then you will have no fear and can dwell in the ultimate dimension, nirvana, right here and now. You don't have to die in order to reach nirvana. When you dwell in your true nature, you are already dwelling in nirvana. We have our historical dimension but we also have our ultimate dimension, just as the Buddha does.

In this introductory chapter, the *Lotus Sutra* reveals to us these two dimensions. The Buddha Shakyamuni is none other than the Buddha Sun and Moon Glow—and all the other cosmic Buddhas that have appeared in various forms to teach the Dharma from beginningless time.

THREE

Skillful Means

THE SECOND CHAPTER of the *Lotus Sutra* is called "Expedient Devices." The Sanskrit term *upaya* is often translated in English as "skillful means." Skillful means are the various skillful ways we can use to fulfill our intentions and manifest our practice. This chapter is the real beginning of the *Lotus Sutra* in that it serves as the foundation for the entire sutra. If we can understand the foundational teaching of skillful means we will be able to grasp the whole of the sutra.

The chapter begins as Shakyamuni Buddha emerges from his samadhi and says to Shariputra, "The wisdom of the Buddha is profound and incalculable. Shravakas or pratyekabuddhas cannot achieve this wisdom." This is a very important detail. The Buddha has just come out of a deep state of meditative concentration and is about to begin delivering this most important Mahayana sutra. Whom does he choose to address at this moment? Not one of the great bodhisattvas, such as Manjushri or Maitreya, but his loyal disciple, the bhikshu Shariputra. In the *Vimalakirtinirdesha Sutra*, Shariputra is held in low regard and made an object of denigration. He represents all the shortcomings of the Hinayana tradition. But now, in the *Lotus Sutra*, he is the object of the Buddha's care and love. In this sutra, Shariputra represents the fourfold community of monks, nuns, laymen, and laywomen to whom the Buddha will transmit the teachings for future generations. Right away we can see how the *Lotus Sutra* aims to reconcile the two traditions.

The Buddha then describes in some detail the profound insight that is "without measure and without obstruction," the wisdom and understanding he has learned and practiced according to the immeasurable methods of countless other Buddhas. Only a Buddha can perfect and realize the insight into the suchness, the true nature, of all *dharmas* (phenomena)—the suchness of their marks (outer appearance), their nature, their substance, their powers, their functions, their causes and conditions, their effects, their retribution, and their ultimate origin. These are called "the ten suchnesses." Many scholars and Dharma masters say that this passage contains the basic philosophy of the *Lotus Sutra*, and they have spent a lot of ink and paper and time analyzing it in great detail. But the meaning of the ten suchnesses can be distilled into one thing: the Buddha's wisdom is very deep and with this insight he is able to see the true nature, the ultimate reality of everything—all dharmas—in time and in space, in the phenomenal world as well as in the ultimate dimension.

The insight of the Buddha is infinitely deep, and not easily understood. Those who are still at the level of the shravakas or pratyekabuddhas cannot fathom this profound insight of the Buddha. Whatever eyes you use to look at the Buddha, you will see the Buddha only through those eyes. If you are driven by craving and look at others through those eyes, everyone you see will seem to you to be full of craving also. If you feel angry, and regard others with eyes of anger and small-mindedness, then you will see everyone as angry and small-minded too. So if you look at the Buddha through the eyes of a shravaka or pratyekabuddha, you will not be able to see the real Buddha as he is, you will see the Buddha only as a shravaka or pratyekabuddha. But the Buddha's insight is much greater than that.

After the Buddha has described this great insight, he says to Shariputra, "Cease, we need speak no more. What is the point of speaking about these things, when people of the world will not be able to understand them?" The seeming reluctance of the Buddha to continue to teach is also a skillful means. The very precious teachings cannot be given too readily, because then they will lose their true value. A Dharma teacher has to be very careful. He or she should not present the Buddhadharma to just anyone but should only teach those whose practice and understanding have ripened to the point where they will be able to receive and put into practice the teachings they are given. Among the assembly gathered around the Buddha, there were those who did not yet have the capacity to receive these new teachings. Some would reject or oppose them. For a Dharma teacher giving a Dharma talk, it is always like this. There will always be some who oppose your ideas.

The Buddha understood that in the audience that day there were some who were not yet ripe, who did not yet have the capacity to receive the truth, and seeing the harm they would bring on themselves by opposing the wonderful Dharma of the *Lotus Sutra*, the Buddha says, "Let us speak no more. This teaching is very rare, very deep, difficult to understand, and difficult to accept. Only a Buddha can realize this teaching."

Hearing this, Shariputra kneels down, joins his palms, and asks the Buddha again, "I beg you, World-Honored One, to expound this matter. Why have you so earnestly praised this very profound and subtle Dharma, so difficult to understand?" But again the Buddha refused, saying, "If I preach this matter, then many people in the worlds, including gods, humans, and asuras, will be seized by fear. And those bhikshus who believe they are already enlightened and do not need to learn anymore will fall into the abyss of doubt and arrogance." Then he spoke this gatha:

> *Cease, cease! No need to speak.*
> *My Dharma is subtle and hard to imagine.*
> *Those of overwhelming pride,*
> *If they hear it, shall surely neither revere it nor believe in it.*[4]

But Shariputra refuses to give up. He entreats the Buddha again, and yet again to preach the wonderful Dharma, for the sake of the fourfold assembly. Shariputra is the advocate for all sincere disciples, and since he has asked the Buddha three times, according to custom, the Buddha cannot refuse and agrees to teach the wonderful Dharma. Immediately upon hearing this, five thousand people stand up, bow respectfully, and leave the assembly. This may seem strange but in fact it often happens. During a public talk, when I come on stage and announce the subject of my talk, very often a number of people will stand up and walk out because they don't want to hear a talk on that subject. After the five thousand had departed, the Buddha said, "The assembly has no more branches or leaves, it has only firm fruit. Shariputra, it is just as well that such arrogant ones as these have withdrawn. Now listen well, for I will preach to you."

Reading this, we may feel some dismay. It does not seem in keeping with the spirit of the Mahayana for the Buddha to dismiss those who left the assembly as unworthy of receiving the teachings. This is a shortcoming of the *Lotus Sutra* that we have not yet seen. The principle message of the *Lotus Sutra* is that all living beings have Buddha nature. Quite naturally, from this point of view, those of the two vehicles, shravakas and pratyekabuddhas, can also become a Buddha. Monks, nuns, laymen and laywomen, children—all have the capacity for Buddhahood. So this passage may reflect more of the spirit of the earlier Mahayana sutras that were highly critical of the Hinayana path. It was in order to address such shortcomings as this in the *Lotus Sutra* that new chapters were later added.

But there is another aspect of this passage, which reveals another kind of skillful means of the Buddha. Those who left the assembly did not feel there was anything more they could learn. With such an attitude, they would not be able to receive the true meaning of the profound teachings the Buddha was about to deliver. Knowing this, the Buddha says that it is just as well, because if someone is not able to receive a teaching's true meaning, that teaching may do more harm than good. It is very important that the hearer of a teaching be appropriately prepared to receive its true import, its deepest insight—otherwise they may fall into doubt and refuse to accept the teaching, which would be more harmful for them than not hearing that teaching at all. Later on, when the time is right and their practice and insight has ripened sufficiently, they will be able to receive the teaching.

Now the Buddha begins to teach the wonderful Dharma. He explains that all the Tathagatas that appear throughout space and time—past, present, and future—do so only in order to open up the Buddhas' great insight, demonstrate that insight, and help beings to awaken and enter the path of the Dharma so that they too can attain Buddhahood. In order to bring all beings to the path of the Dharma, these Buddhas employ "incalculable expedient devices," offering the teaching in various forms that are suited to different personality types and temperaments. The teachings may be given in the form of discourses in prose (sutras); discourses in verse (geya); or short verses (gatha); in tales of the Buddha's former lives (jataka); miracle tales (adbhuta); in the teaching of causes and conditions (nidana); in parables (aupamya); quotes (itivrittaka); or dialogue (upadesha).[5] These many different forms of teaching are a skillful means used by the Buddha to teach people with different levels of understanding.

Here the Buddha reveals one of the most important insights of the Lotus Sutra. The various skillful means used by the Buddhas to teach beings are all aimed at one goal: to bring everyone, regardless of their spiritual capacity or attainment, whether they are followers of the shravaka or pratyekabuddha paths, monastic or layperson, man, woman, or child, into the bodhisattva path. Before, the historical Buddha Shakyamuni had taught such concepts as attainment of the three stages leading to arhatship, personal nirvana, and the path of individual enlightenment through direct observation of dependent co-arising. These are the two vehicles of the Hinayana, the shravakayana and the pratyekabuddhayana. Now, in the Lotus Sutra, the Buddha reveals that the teachings of the two vehicles were only an expedient device used to reach those of limited spiritual capacity or aspiration.

Some people want only to find relief from their own suffering. They feel it is all they can do to try to liberate themselves, and so they take up the practice and attend a retreat or two at Plum Village, and receive the benefit of that. This is the shravaka path. Then there are some practitioners who are able to get a direct insight into the nature of the twelve links (nidanas) of dependent co-arising and attain freedom for themselves, but they do not wish to teach or guide others. This is the path of the pratyekabuddha. Others have a wider aspiration. They hope that by practicing the Dharma they will be able to organize Dharma communities and share the benefits of the practice with many people. Rather than just enjoying their own attainment, they want to share the fruits of their practice with others. This is the bodhisattva path. So when the time is ripe the Buddha reveals the path of the One Vehicle (ekayana), the Great Vehicle of the Mahayana, which embraces all three of these paths—the shravakayana, pratyekabuddhayana, and bodhisattvayana.[6] The One Vehicle teaching says you can do more—you can arrive at the fruit of the highest awakening, become a Buddha, and help many other beings across the river of suffering to the shore of freedom.

The Buddha affirms that the two vehicles are worthy paths, but they are not the ultimate teaching because they are not founded on *bodhichitta*, the great aspiration to dedicate one's own practice and realization to help bring liberation, peace, and joy to the whole world.[7] The paths of the shravakas and pratyekabuddhas were taught only as a skillful means through which practitioners can grow spiritually to the point where they will be able to generate the great aspiration to become a Buddha and enter the One Vehicle.

The Buddha taught these three vehicles to respond to the different levels and capacities of beings, the different causes and conditions, and the different times and situations in which the teachings were given. The three-vehicles teaching is a skillful means in the historical dimension. In terms of the ultimate dimension, however, the Buddha always aims to reveal the deepest meaning, the absolute truth. The reason for all the Tathagatas' appearance in the world is to guide living beings to the ultimate truth of the One Vehicle, which is also called the Buddha vehicle—opening up, pointing out, awakening to, and entering the insight of the Buddha.[8] So the philosophy of the One Vehicle revealed in the *Lotus Sutra* has been called "opening up the three to the one" or "gathering the three and returning them to the one." The teaching of the three vehicles is but a skillful means; in fact, there is only One Vehicle. The Buddha says in a verse:

> *Within the Buddha lands of the ten directions*
> *There is the Dharma of only One Vehicle.*
> *There are not two, nor are there yet three,*
> *Save where the Buddha, preaching by resort to expedients,*
> *And by merely borrowing provisional names and words,*
> *Draws the beings to him.*[9]

This passage is considered the essence of the second chapter of the *Lotus Sutra*. With this insight, the sutra achieves something that all previous Mahayana sutras had not yet been able to do. It reconciles and unifies the teachings of the three vehicles into the One Vehicle, the great vehicle that has the capacity to carry all beings to the shore of liberation. This is the heart of the wonderful Dharma, and it is for this reason that the *Lotus Sutra* is regarded as the "King of Sutras"—not because it expresses more profound or mystical theories, but because it reunites all the disciples and paths of practice into the one great family of the Buddha.

ᕍ FOUR

One Vehicle

THE NEXT SEVEN CHAPTERS of the *Lotus Sutra*, Chapter Three through Chapter Nine, are called "the seven chapters of clear exposition," and they serve to further clarify skillful means. At the very end of Chapter Two, the Buddha says in verse,

> *All of you, knowing now*
> *That the Buddhas, the Teachers of the Ages,*
> *In accord with what is peculiarly appropriate have recourse to expedient devices,*
> *Need have no more doubts or uncertainties.*
> *Your hearts shall give rise to great joy,*
> *Since you know that you yourselves shall become Buddhas.*[10]

Chapter Three, "Parable," opens with Shariputra's response to this great revelation. At first, on hearing the profound and wonderful teachings, Shariputra harbored doubts, thinking that Mara had appeared as the Buddha to give false teachings. The idea that all living beings have Buddha nature and the capacity for Buddhahood, that there are not two or three vehicles but only one Buddha vehicle, was almost too much for him to imagine. The impact of these profound revelations must have been quite intense. Shariputra's doubting the truth of these revelations is representative of that of many followers of the early Buddhist tradition, who thought that all Mahayana sutras were actually put forth by Mara to confuse listeners and lead them astray. This passage in the sutra is a vestige of this view.[11]

The *Lotus Sutra* describes how once Shariputra looked deeply and carefully, he saw that it really was the Buddha who was giving these wonderful and deep teachings. He "danced for joy" and immediately cast off all his doubts. Though previously he had followed the path of the shravakas, on hearing the teaching of the One Vehicle he realizes that he too has the capacity for Buddhahood and his mind gives rise to bodhichitta:

> *Of a certainty I shall become a Buddha,*
> *Revered by gods and men;*
> *I shall turn the unexcelled Dharma-wheel,*
> *Teaching and converting bodhisattvas.*[12]

Shariputra has determined to become a Buddha, and when he makes this proclamation he has already entered the bodhisattva path. Hearing this the Buddha said, "Shariputra, in past lives you studied and practiced with me, and I taught you the bodhisattva way. But in this lifetime you forgot it and, following the path of the shravaka, believed you had reached the final goal of your practice, nirvana. Now, through teaching this Lotus Blossom of the Fine Dharma, I am able to reestablish you on the bodhisattva path. In the future you will become the Buddha Flower Glow (Padmaprabha) in a Buddha land called Free of Defilements (Viraja). You will do as I do, and teach the three vehicles to guide living beings, and finally you will also teach the One Vehicle, just as I am teaching now."

This passage is a prediction. The Buddha is able to recognize the innate capacities of a person and see what that person will be able to realize in the future, and which path he or she needs to take in order to realize those capacities. All living beings are able to become a Buddha but they all become Buddha in a different way, and each Buddha teaches in a different way. A wise teacher, when he or she looks at their disciples, is able to see which path each disciple will follow in the future and the realization they will attain, and with this knowledge the teacher can help their disciples have more confidence and follow the right path. Giving a prediction is a transmission of spiritual energy from teacher to disciple.

Now, when the other members of the assembly witnessed the Buddha's prediction of Shariputra's Buddhahood, they also rejoiced, because they understood that if Shariputra is able to become Buddha then they, and all living beings, also have the capacity for Buddhahood. This creates a feeling of great joy and enormous confidence in everyone's heart. But fearing that there are still some among the fourfold assembly who have doubts, Shariputra asks the Buddha to use his skillful means to further explicate the teaching of the One Vehicle. So the Buddha offers the parable of the burning house.

A phrase that appears often in Buddhist texts is, "The three realms are in disturbance, just like a house on fire." According to classical Buddhist thought, the three realms are three levels of samsaric existence: the realm of desire (*kamadhatu*), the ordinary world we inhabit, where beings are subject to the three poisons of greed, anger, and delusion; the realm of form (*rupadhatu*), a higher realm of existence in which beings have severed some attachments; and the realm of formlessness (*arupadhatu*), the highest realm of samsaric existence in which beings are free of attachment to form. Even though the higher two of the three realms may offer some respite from the three poisons, all three are still samsara. None of the three realms can provide real peace or security. They are like a burning house, full of traps and dangers.

Imagine a group of chickens in a cage. They fight each other to get the corn and they fight over whether the corn or the rice tastes better. And all the while they are competing with each other over a few kernels of corn or grains of rice, they are unaware that in a few hours they will be taken to the slaughterhouse. We too live in a world full of insecurity, but we do not see it because we are so caught up in our craving and delusions.

The parable given by the Buddha tells of a wealthy merchant who has many acres of land and many servants, and a large house where many people live. But the house has only one door. The house is full of dangers and in fact is not a very safe place to live. One day a fire breaks out. The merchant sees that the house is on fire and he knows that it is a very dangerous situation, because his children are playing inside the house. The merchant loves his children very much and does not want them to die The merchant cries out, "Children, run out quickly! The house is on fire, it will collapse and you will all be burned!"

But the children continue to play. The children are so caught up in their games that they don't even realize the house is burning. When they finally hear the merchant yelling at them to run out of the house, they ignore him. They are not afraid. They say, "Why do we have to go outside? Where's the fire? What's the danger?" They were so enjoying their games and distractions that they didn't want to leave the house, even though it was about to collapse.

The merchant was very sad but, in his sadness, he was able to find a way to help. He thought, "How foolish are these children, how attached to their games! I will use a skillful means to break their absorption in their games in order to have a chance to save them."

Knowing that his children liked to play with carts he called out, "My children, I have brought for you a number of very beautiful carts. Some of them are pulled by goats, some by deer, some by oxen. They are all different colors and shapes. If you come out of the house, each of you can have one of these carts."

When the children heard this they were very excited and they jostled with one another trying to push through the door of the house to get to the carts. But once they were outside, they saw only one very beautiful cart, pulled by a magnificent white ox. There were no deer carts or goat carts—only this one kind of cart. But once they saw the beautiful ox cart pulled by a white ox, all the children immediately wanted to climb into it.

When we hear this story, we may think it's just a children's story and that it does not really have anything to do with our lives. But if we look more deeply into our minds and the state of mind of those around us, we see that this parable expresses the truth about our situation. We are full of craving, always running after things. We want to become a director or president of a company, we want to buy a beautiful car or a nice house, or go on an exotic vacation. We do not see that the world we are living in, driven by craving and delusion, is like a burning house.

After relating this parable, the Buddha said, "Shariputra, the merchant promised his children that they would have many kinds of carts but in the end he gave only one kind of cart, pulled by a white ox. Why did he do that? Because his beloved children deserved only the best kind of cart; only the best was worthy of his love for them. Therefore he gave them the most luxurious cart drawn by a white ox. Would you say that he told a lie?"

Shariputra said, "No, we cannot say that he was telling a lie. Out of his love for them, the merchant gave his children the most precious thing. The reason he offered different kinds of carts is because he wanted to give his children something they would like."

The Buddha said, "That is correct. Among the merchant's children were some who liked goat carts, some who liked deer carts, and some who liked ox carts. So he said that for those who like the goat cart there is a goat cart, for those who like the deer cart there is a deer cart. He offered these different kinds of carts to make his children happy but in the end because he wanted only to give them the best kind of cart, the most precious cart, the most luxurious cart, he gave them the white ox cart. Living beings are like this. Some have a liking for the shravakayana, some for the pratyekabuddhayana, some for the bodhisattvayana. But in the end the Buddha gives living beings the most precious vehicle, the One Vehicle that transcends all other vehicles, the Buddha vehicle. Although I have spoken of the three vehicles, there is in fact only One Vehicle."

The sutra tells us that the Buddha says to himself, "I am the Father of the beings; I must rescue them from their woes and troubles and give them the joy of incalculable and limitless Buddha-wisdom." The word "Father" here is a symbol of the Buddha's love and concern for his children, all living beings. A father will use any means to rescue his children from a dangerous situation. That is how the Buddha feels about us. He sees how we are attached to our games, living in an illusion, and because of this we are not able to see the danger of our situation. So out of his love for his children, he uses various methods to lead them out of suffering.

A disciple of the Buddha is the spiritual child of the Buddha. Our parents bring us into the world, they give us our physical body. When we come to the practice we are reborn into our spiritual life, thanks to the Buddha. In the sutras it is said that the disciple is "born from the mouth of the Buddha." From the mouth of the Buddha comes the sound of the true teachings, and from the true teachings comes our spiritual life. This beautiful image of the Buddha as the spiritual father of all beings is a symbol of his great love. The idea of "father" here symbolizes only a heart of love that is able to embrace all beings. It is not about authority or domination. The father does not fly into a rage, he does not punish us or send us down into hell. His only function is to love. And because the father loves his children he uses many different ways—skillful means—to save them from danger. The verses say:

> *Even though the Buddhas, the World-Honored Ones,*
> *Resort to expedient devices,*
> *The living beings whom they convert*
> *Are all bodhisattvas.*[13]

All the Buddhas throughout space and time, not just the present Shakyamuni Buddha, use these skillful means to help bring living beings out of the burning house. The Buddha's original teachings—the Four Noble Truths, the Eightfold Path, the Three Dharma Seals, the shravaka path of arhatship, dependent co-arising, and so on were taught as skillful means to reach those who did not yet have the capacity to accept the direct teaching of the wonderful Dharma, which is the essential Buddha nature of all beings, their capacity for Buddhahood—in fact, their assurance of Buddhahood.[14] Once living beings are able to enter the One Vehicle, they are all bodhisattvas. These two ideas in this chapter of the *Lotus Sutra* are very important.

The teachings of the shravakayana—the Four Noble Truths, and so on—were taught to help people free themselves from delusion and get some relief from their suffering. The fruit of this path, nirvana, literally means to "blow out, extinguish," just as one blows out a candle flame. The idea was that you would leave the burning house of samsara once and for all, never to be reborn. But leaving behind one's delusions and thinking of nirvana as extinction are not yet the authentic liberation. It is the first part of liberation but it is not the whole picture. The idea of nirvana as extinction is a skillful means teaching to bring people into the path of practice.

The Mahayana proposed a different understanding of nirvana, which is not separate from our existence in the world. True nirvana is possible in the here and now when we are able to get in touch with the ultimate dimension of reality. Just as a wave does not have to die in order to live in its ultimate dimension of water, we do not have to "extinguish" ourselves in order to reach nirvana, When we get in touch with our true nature, our ultimate dimension, we are freed from fears of existence and nonexistence. We know that "samsara" and "nirvana" are just distinctions in the realm of the historical dimension, and no such distinction exists in the ultimate dimension. As bodhisattvas, assured of Buddhahood, we ride joyfully on the waves of birth and death, abiding fearlessly in samsara to help guide others to liberation.

The Buddha says in a gatha:

> I am the Dharma King,
>   With respect to the Dharma acting completely at will.[15]

The Buddha, the Dharma King, grasps the true nature, the ultimate dimension, of all things (dharmas) and therefore has the ability to use various skillful means to teach beings in the phenomenal realm—this world of form and appearances called samsara. The various teachings are Dharma doors,[16] and a Buddha is someone who can enter any of these Dharma gateways at will and use them in a very free and skillful way, just as a great poet knows how to use words with great artistry and skill. So the teachings may appear in different forms, but ultimately they all lead to the One Vehicle, the Buddha vehicle, in which all beings realize their innate Buddha nature. This is absolute freedom in the field of time and space, nirvana right in the realm of samsara, and this is the great insight of the Mahayana.

CR FIVE

The Destitute Son

*L*otus Sutra Chapter Four, "Belief and Understanding," also furthers the teaching of skillful means through an example given in a parable. Here it is not the Buddha but four of his disciples, Subhuti, Mahakatyayana, Mahakashyapa, and Mahamaudgalyayana, who tell the story. Thanks to the Buddha's teaching of the *Lotus Sutra*, these four monks realized awakening. They knelt before the Buddha and addressed him, "We belong to the shravakayana. Well-advanced in age, we thought we had already attained nirvana and therefore had no further tasks to perform. We did not have the intention to become a fully enlightened being, a Buddha. But now that the Buddha has opened our eyes to the truth and explained the matter to us clearly, we have gained the inexhaustible energy of the bodhisattva. We wish to show our gratitude to you by offering a parable to the assembly." Then the monks related the parable of the destitute son.

There was a man who when very young had run away from his family and had become impoverished and destitute. For fifty years he wandered far and wide, trying to find a way to make a living. Then one day, having long since forgotten the land of his birth and his family, he returned to his native country unaware that he had done so. His father had become a successful, wealthy merchant. Over the years he had always thought lovingly of his lost son and regretted that his son had run away from home at such an early age. With no one to inherit his fortune when he died, the merchant believed that his wealth would be scattered. But he had never spoken to anyone of his situation and this made his feeling of loss and regret even greater.

The destitute son came to the palace of this rich man one day to look for work as a laborer. Peering in from the doorway, he saw the man sitting on a lion throne, resting his feet on a footstool of precious materials. Many brahmans and nobles and other rich merchants were respectfully gathered around the wealthy man. He was so rich that members of the government and even of the royal family visited in order to stay on good terms with him. His palace was opulent, with curtains of precious jewels, beautiful garlands of flowers, and perfumed water sprinkling in fountains. Seeing this, the destitute son asked himself, "Why have I come here? It's very dangerous. They could arrest me and put me in prison. People like me are not welcome in such luxurious palaces." So he left.

While he had been at the doorway, however, the wealthy merchant immediately recognized him as his son. He was very moved, and in his excitement he ordered one of his servants to run after the man and bring him back. But when the son saw a servant from the palace coming after him, he became afraid. He said to the servant, "Sir, I have not done anything wrong. I have not offended against anyone. Why are you arresting me?" But the servant had to carry out his orders so he grabbed the son and forced him back to the house. Panicked, the destitute son thought, "This is the end. Now I have been arrested and they will execute me." He was so afraid that he lost consciousness and collapsed.

At that moment the father saw his mistake. Though he had acted out of love, he understood that the method he had used to get his son back was much too forceful. We too love people in this way. Sometimes the intensity of our feelings can make our beloved feel suffocated. We want so much to express our feelings of love to them that it can be too much. So sometimes, even though we may love someone very much, we have to be careful not to frighten or overwhelm the object of our love with our strong feelings. When the merchant saw that his son had passed out from fear, he regretted very much what he had done. He sprinkled some water on the man's face to revive him. When the son came around the merchant did not burst out saying that he was the man's father and profess his love. Instead, he told him, "I've made a mistake; I've arrested you wrongly. I thought you had committed an offense but in fact you have not. You are an honest man and you are free to go wherever you want to go."

This is the true meaning of love. When we truly love someone we have to let him or her be free. If we tie someone up in our love, even though the bonds are made from our love it is not true love. When the destitute son heard that he was free, he was so happy. In all his life he had never felt as happy as at that moment. He had not gained anything new yet he was overjoyed, because he had regained the most precious thing on this earth—his freedom.

The merchant was using skillful means. He knew if he tried to bring his lost son back to him too quickly or abruptly the man would not be able to accept it. So he instructed two men to disguise themselves in dirty, ripped clothing, as if they too were destitute, follow the son, and befriend him. They would ask the son to go with them to perform some work and pay him a little money. Nevertheless, the merchant instructed that his son should be given the most lowly work to do, like sweeping up excrement, carting away rubbish, and so on, the kind of work that those of even small means would avoid. The merchant knew that his son, having lived his whole life in extreme poverty and having no means to better himself, would not believe himself capable of anything but the humblest kind of work. Naturally, when he was given low work like this to do, he knew that he was capable of it and thought himself lucky. He did not need anything more, and he did not aspire toward any greater happiness.

A couple of months later the destitute son was working near the wealthy merchant's house. The father still missed his son very much. So he altered his appearance himself. He took off all the gold, silver, and jewels, and traded his fine clothes for ordinary ones. Then he approached his son in order to become acquainted with him. Although the father had disguised himself as an ordinary worker, he still had a nobleman's manner and authority. When he met his destitute son he was very kind and solicitous. He asked him, "Where do you come from? How long have you been working here? Do you have enough to eat? Are you given a decent wage?" The merchant's great love for his lost son is revealed in these questions. And he said to his son, "Although you are not actually my son, I regard all those who work for me as my own sons, so you do not have any reason to be afraid of me."

The merchant used these skillful means in order to diminish his son's fear and feeling of inferiority and build up his confidence little by little. And in this way, he became close to his son. The merchant praised his strength, loyalty, honesty, and respectful manner toward others. Gradually, the son's affection and trust toward the merchant grew. The merchant did not reveal to the man that he was his son, because he knew that the destitute son would not have believed it. So the merchant told him instead, "I look on you as my adopted son." The man was extremely happy. In all his life he had never had someone treat him as kindly as he was being treated now. He had become the trusted assistant to the master of the house. He could come and to go as he liked without fear. He was given a number of tasks of great importance. But he still believed that he was adopted, a trusted servant of the master but not his direct descendant. Even though the destitute son had taken on the role of a manager—he made important decisions and dealt with large sums of money—nevertheless he still had a servant's attitude of mind.

Here we begin to see the meaning of this parable. The small vehicle teachings say that the shravaka disciples cannot realize the profound insight and become a Buddha, as Shakyamuni did. So the shravakas lacked confidence and did not believe they possessed or could cultivate the spiritual capacity of a bodhisattva and lead others to liberation, they could only attain nirvana for themselves. Only the goat or deer carts were suitable to them; they did not yet believe themselves worthy of the glorious white ox cart of the Buddha.

In the parable, the wealthy merchant (the Buddha) cannot right away reveal to the destitute son (the shravakas) that he is his father. So he carefully builds up his son's confidence and draws him closer. Eventually, the destitute son will be able to realize and accept that he is the worthy heir of a vast fortune. But a truth, especially such a profound truth about our own nature that we had never before thought possible, must be revealed at the right moment. Revealing a truth at an inappropriate moment, when the hearer is not yet mentally or spiritually prepared, can cause great harm. This is why the Buddha first gave the small vehicle teaching and only later, after his disciples had mastered those teachings and their practice had ripened sufficiently, did he reveal the teachings of the bodhisattvayana to them. Had he done so earlier, they would have rejected the teachings. The Buddha used skillful means to deliver the right teaching at just the right time in order to eventually lead all his disciples to the One Vehicle.

In the parable, the merchant also had to wait for the right moment to tell the truth. Slowly and gradually, he had built up his son's confidence in himself as someone who is worthy and capable. When the merchant fell seriously ill and knew that he was nearing the end of his life, he realized that the time had come to reveal the true nature of their relationship. He organized a gathering attended by the king and royal family, various dignitaries, military officials, scholars, and others. This detail reveals that the merchant wielded great power and influence. Then he brought the destitute son before the assembly and said, "Though you know this man only as the manager of my household, in fact he is my son." In his whole life the man had never dared think that he was the son of a great man of tremendous power, influence, and wealth. But now the time had come and the truth could be presented without doing any harm. The son hears and accepts the truth, and realizes "that which had not yet been realized."

This point in the parable is equivalent to the moment of the Buddha's delivery of the *Lotus Sutra*, when he reveals that everyone possesses Buddha nature and has the capacity for Buddhahood. And the destitute son's state of mind, his realization, is the same as that of the shravakas when they hear and accept that they too are the real children of the Buddha, bodhisattvas on the way to Buddhahood. They no longer believe they can achieve their own liberation only but know they are capable of much more. Their doubts are lifted and they rejoice:

> *We this day*
> *Have gained something we have never had before,*
> *Something which, though never before hoped for,*
> *Yet now has come into our possession of its own accord.*
> *As that poor son*
> *Gained incalculable gems,*
> *So, O World Honored One, have we now*
> *Gained the Path and the Fruit....*

We now
   Are truly voice-hearers,
Taking the voice of the Buddha Path
   And causing all to hear it.[17]

This parable presented by the bhikshus Subhuti, Katyayana, Kashyapa, and Maudgalyayana is aimed at opening the eyes of their fellow disciples, who believed that their practice to attain individual liberation was quite enough. They felt they had achieved all that there was to achieve. Although they had heard the wonderful Dharma of the *Lotus Sutra*, they still did not believe in it. They had heard the Buddha speak of the bodhisattva practice of guiding all beings to liberation, yet still they did not feel drawn to it because they had not yet given birth to the great aspiration, bodhichitta. But the four bhikshus knew that their destiny was much greater. So they offered this parable to their brothers and sisters to reveal to them their true destiny as inheritors of the noble career of the Buddha.

✼ SIX

Dharma Rain

IN ANCIENT INDIA, medicines were derived from leaves and plants, and the name of *Lotus Sutra* Chapter Five, "Medicinal Herbs," refers to this fact. This chapter offers another example of the Buddha's skillful means. The Buddha describes to Kashyapa how he looks into the hearts of living beings, and based on that perception he offers the most appropriate and skillful teaching—just as a good physician prescribes the right medicine for each person's ailment.

Whether a Dharma talk succeeds or fails does not depend on the teacher's eloquence or on whether their knowledge of the Dharma is profound or superficial. The transformative power of a teaching depends entirely on the teacher's understanding and clear perception of the psychological state and situation of those who will receive it. A Dharma talk must always be appropriate in two ways: it must accord perfectly with the spirit of the Dharma and it must also respond perfectly to the situation in which it is given. If it only corresponds perfectly with the teachings but does not meet the needs of the listeners, it's not a good Dharma talk; it's not appropriate.

The Dharma is like a powerful lamp, helping people to see deeply into their situation and releasing them from suffering. When a teaching touches real concerns, real suffering, it can unblock the obstacles and difficulties that are there in the mind of the listener. When you hear a Dharma talk that is appropriate in these two ways, faithful to both the true teaching and the actual conditions and situation of the listeners, you have the feeling that it is directed to you personally. It is as if the teacher has seen right into your heart and is speaking to you and you alone. When many people have this feeling, that is the mark of a skillful Dharma talk.

43

The teacher gets insight from looking deeply into the situation of his students, observing and listening to them in order to understand them. When we can understand them, then the teaching we offer will be a good influence on their lives. With regard to one person, a skillful teacher may give a particular teaching, while for another person he or she may teach something quite different. There is a well-known story of a Chinese Ch'an master who, when asked by a student whether a dog has Buddha nature, answered yes. When another student asked him the same question, he said no.

Whether or not beings have Buddha nature is not something that can be taught just because we have read it in a sutra or adhere to some abstract principle or theory. A teaching is not merely a set of ideas or information but a tool, a skillful means that can help unblock and liberate those who hear it. Looking deeply into the psychological and spiritual state of the questioner, a teacher may say "yes" because that is the response that will be most beneficial for that person. Yet for another student, he or she may say "no" in order to help their student look more deeply. With some students, we have to speak gently in order to be successful. For others, we have to shout. Using a different approach for different students has nothing to do with personal preference; it is a simply a reflection of the teacher's insight into each student's particular situation.

In this chapter, the Buddha says to Kashyapa, "Bhikshu, you should know that the Tathagata is the Dharma King. If the Tathagata says something then those words are not false, they are always true. If the Tathagata says something exists, that is true. If the Tathagata says something does not exist, that is also true. If the Tathagata teaches the Mahayana, it is true. And if the Tathagata teaches the Hinayana, it is also true." From his great wisdom, the Buddha gave teachings in the form that was most appropriate for the listeners at the time. But all the teachings of the Buddha have the capacity to bring us to the level of *sarvajñana*, the highest absolute wisdom, universal wisdom. Looking deeply, the Tathagata is able to know the circumstances of all living beings. He knows the ultimate result of all the teachings. His knowledge of all dharmas is complete, without obstacle. And he has the capacity to present his perfect wisdom to all living beings through the skillful means of the various teachings.

In this chapter the Buddha uses the example of medicinal herbs. Throughout the worlds there are innumerable valleys, fields, and gardens that contain countless species of plants. Every species has its own name and character, its own life cycle, its specific strengths and properties. None is exactly like another. Living beings are the same. They have many different types. The sphere of activities of one person is like this; the social circumstance of another person is like that. Living beings are thus like the innumerable kinds of plants that grow in different environments.

One day the clouds came and covered the entire cosmos, and rain fell on all the species of plants. Some plants were very small with slim branches, some were very large with broad leaves, and some were neither small nor large. There were so many species, so many types of plants, yet they all benefited fully from the rain, each according to its own needs and capacity.

The teachings of the Buddha are like this. The rain of the Dharma falls not just on one class or type of human being. Whether they are shravakas, pratyekabuddhas, or bodhisattvas, monastics or laypeople, nobles (brahmans) or peasants, workers or warriors (*kshatriyas*), male or female, child, youth, adult, or elder—all beings benefit from the Tathagata's teachings. The Dharma is universal and has the capacity to serve all kinds of people, not just one social class, one nation, or one kind of understanding such as that of the shravakayana or the bodhisattvayana.

Living beings cannot see into their own true nature right away, but the Buddha can. The Tathagata looks deeply into different beings, their forms, their essence, and their innate dispositions, and so is able to offer the Dharma in the way that is most beneficial to them. Seeing that one kind of disciple will best be able to follow a particular path of practice, the Buddha opens that Dharma gate. Mahayana sutras often mention "84,000 Dharma doors," which is a way of saying that there are an infinite number of teachings and methods by which living beings may be liberated.

The verses describe the Dharma as being "of a single flavor." Just as the rain has one function, one effect—to nourish all the different species of plants and cause them to grow—the different teachings offered by the Tathagata as skillful means have but one taste—the taste of liberation and universal wisdom that delivers all beings to the realm of peace and joy.

The Magic City

THE PREVIOUS THREE CHAPTERS of the *Lotus Sutra* were in the form of parables. *Lotus Sutra* Chapter Seven, "Parable of the Conjured City," is also in this form, so in order to give our discussion a clearer flow, we will first look into the parable given in Chapter Seven, and then afterwards discuss the three chapters on prophecy.[18]

The parable of the magic city tells of a long and dangerous journey. A group started out on a journey of 500 *yojanas* to seek a great treasure.[19] Led by a very skillful guide, well-versed in the topography of the region, they traveled through remote desert lands full of many kinds of fearsome creatures. The guide is called "the teacher of the path, the one who shows us the way."

The journey was long and many dangers and misfortunes befell the group. When they had not yet traversed even half the distance, the people grew weary. They lost all their energy and strength, and felt they could go on no longer. They thought that it would be best to turn around and go back home. Many of us have experienced similar feelings of discouragement and hopelessness. Perhaps we have many things to do and we don't know how we are going to complete all our tasks. We may have started out with a lot of energy and enthusiasm, but along the way we encountered obstacles and setbacks, and we began to feel that we could not continue.

At this point, just as the people were about to give up, the guide told them, "Keep on just a little bit longer, we will soon arrive at our destination." In fact, the guide knew that they still had far to go but he used skillful means to conjure a magical city. Then he told them, "A short way ahead there is a fine city where we can refresh ourselves and regain our strength." When they heard this, the people rallied themselves enough to push on to the city. There, they were able to eat, drink, bathe, and rest until they felt completely well again. And because they felt so happy and well in that city, they all wanted to stay there and not continue the difficult journey. They said to themselves, "If we carry on it will just mean more hardship and danger. We have really accomplished quite enough just to arrive at this point."

They had forgotten that their aim was not just to enjoy their comfort in the magical city but to find the treasure storehouse of precious jewels. When the guide said it was time to continue the journey, everyone said, "No, let's stay here. What's the point of going on? It will only make us weary again." There are people like this in our own time. They say, "I have practiced and have gained some of the fruits of the practice. I have more mindfulness and ease in my life, I feel happier and more at peace. That is enough. Why should I continue to work so hard to establish a practice center and organize retreats for others? It is difficult and tiring. You have to meet and deal with all kinds of people, some of whom are very hard to be with. It's easier just to stay home." Someone who thinks like this is caught in the magic city.

So the guide, the teacher of the way, used skillful means again. He said, "Do you really think this city is sufficient to meet your real needs? As wonderful as it is to stay and enjoy life here, this is just a resting place for us. It is not the true land of freedom. If you continue on to the Jewel Mountain you will not have wasted your life." The guide used every method to help people increase their willingness to continue further on the path, to help them generate the energy to leave their comfortable abode and seek the real treasure storehouse full of precious jewels.

The Buddha is our skillful guide, our teacher of the way. The Buddha gives us just one path, One Vehicle, to arrive at universal wisdom. But when we have gone only halfway we are already worn out. So the Buddha created a magical city—nirvana—the goal of the Hinayana path. Tasting the fruit of individual nirvana, we like it so much that we decide that it is quite enough for us and we do not want anything more.

Underlying this attitude is a kind of inferiority complex. We do not believe that we ourselves can become a Buddha because only such a great being as the Buddha could attain perfect wisdom. Mere humans are not capable of this. In terms of the historical dimension, the Buddha was a human being, like us. But after the Buddha's parinirvana, people very much missed his presence, his personality. Even though he repeatedly warned his disciples, "Don't take refuge in anyone, any person—take refuge only in the Dharma and in yourselves," the Buddha had been a refuge for the Sangha. So they began to envelop him in many layers of mysticism and made him into a deity to worship. They began to believe that the Buddha was unique and he lost his status as a human being. The human dimension of the Buddha is more accessible to us than the deified Buddha that was created after his parinirvana.[20]

The feeling of the shravakayana is that you cannot yourself become a Buddha, you cannot be equal to a Buddha, because the Buddha is too great, he is unique. Along with this belief was the feeling that you don't *need* to become a Buddha, so there is no need to cultivate bodhichitta, the aspiration to attain Buddhahood, in order to help others. You have a lot of suffering and want to stop your suffering, so you concern yourself only with your own safety and liberation. You are satisfied with a small path, a small nirvana.

Out of his compassion and love for us, the Buddha gave the small-vehicle teaching of nirvana in the beginning. But after a time our skillful guide tells us it is time to go farther on the path. Even though many of us may be satisfied to stay and enjoy the peace and bliss of individual nirvana, the Buddha reminds us of our ultimate goal: to arrive at the shore of universal wisdom and then extend a hand to others so that they may cross over to liberation. From the path of shravakayana we continue onto the bodhisattva path of the Mahayana and continue our journey to the end.

৶ EIGHT

Predictions

IN *Lotus Sutra* Chapters Six, Eight, and Nine, the prophecy chapters, the Buddha predicts the future Buddhahood of many kinds of disciples and followers, beginning with his disciples Kashyapa, Subhuti, Katyayana, and Maudgalyayana. These are the four bhikshus who had offered the parable of the destitute son to help their brother and sister shravakas free themselves from doubt once and for all and accept the teaching of the Buddha vehicle. In Chapter Six, "Bestowal of Prophecy," the Buddha predicts that Kashyapa will become the Buddha called Brilliant Glow (Rashmiprabhasa) and establish a glorious Buddha land called Glow Power (Prabhasaprapta). Next, the Buddha predicts Subhuti's Buddhahood as a Buddha called Moon Sign (Shashiketu) who will preside over a Pure Land called Birthplace of Jewels (Ratnasambhava). Katyayana will become a Buddha called Golden Glow (Jambunadaprabhasa), and Maudgalyayana will become the Buddha Sandalwood Fragrance (Tamalapatracandana). The Buddha lands that these four Buddhas will inhabit are described in very beautiful terms: they have all kinds of splendid adornments and are free from all manner of difficulty or pain.

This brief chapter serves to confirm the Buddhahood of these four bhikshus. Thanks to the Buddha's teaching of the Lotus Blossom of the Wonderful Dharma, these former shravakas have now entered the path of the bodhisattva in order to help bring all beings to the shore of liberation, and so their Buddhahood is assured.

In Chapter Eight, "Receipt of Prophecy by Five Hundred Disciples," the Buddha predicts the future Buddhahood of Purna, one of his ten outstanding disciples. His full name is Purnamaitrayaniputra (Son of maitrayana). *Maitrayana*, which was the name of his mother, is

Sanskrit for "the fullness of loving-kindness." He was foremost among the Buddha's senior disciples in giving excellent Dharma talks. Purna was present in the assembly when the Buddha predicted the Buddha-hood of the four bhikshus, and he was so moved by this that he came to stand near the Buddha as he was teaching. Then the Buddha looked at Purna and began to praise his fine qualities and practice, and pre-dicted that he would become the Buddha Dharma Glow (Dharmaprab-hasa) in a Buddha land called Well Purified (Suvishuddha).

In that land there are two kinds of food that are given to the people every day—the food of Dharma Joy and the food of Meditative Delight. Dharma Joy is the feeling of joy we have when we are able to hear and learn about the Dharma. When we listen to a Dharma talk, participate in a Dharma discussion, and study the teachings, it is great joy and it is also a kind of nourishment for us. The food of Dharma Joy belongs to the realm of study, and the food of Meditative Delight, meditative concentration, belongs to the field of practice. When you listen to the teachings with concentration, you are at the same time enjoying the food of Dharma Joy and the food of Meditative Delight. These two expressions, Dharma Joy and Meditative Delight, are taken from a gatha in the *Avatamsaka Sutra*.

After Buddha had predicted Purna's Buddhahood, 1,200 arhats in the assembly thought, "Now the bhikshu Purna has received the prophecy of his Buddhahood. If the Buddha would predict Buddha-hood for all his other disciples, we would be overjoyed." The Buddha was able to know the thoughts in the minds of those in the assembly, and so he predicted Buddhahood for his disciple Kaundinya and 500 other arhats. Kaundinya represents the most senior disciples of the Buddha. He was the eldest of the five ascetics who had practiced with Siddhartha before his attainment of Buddhahood, and who had aban-doned him when, near death, Siddhartha had given up ascetic prac-tice, bathed and took food, and sat under the bodhi tree.[21] After he had attained enlightenment and became the Buddha, he went looking for these five ascetics in order to teach them what he had learned. Though they had rejected him, these five men were so struck by the Buddha's radiant and serene appearance that they agreed to listen to what he had to say. Thus they heard the Buddha's first Dharma talk on the Four

Noble Truths, in the Deer Park at Sarnath, and became the first members of the Buddha's Sangha.

After Kaundinya and the 500 arhats received the prophecy of their Buddhahood, they rejoiced, and then approached the Buddha, bowed deeply in gratitude before him, and offered the following parable of the precious jewel in the robe. A man goes to a friend's house, drinks wine, becomes inebriated, and falls into a sound sleep. The owner of the house has to go far away for a while. Because he loves his friend and wants to take care of him, the man carefully sews a number of valuable jewels into the hem of his friend's cloak as he is sleeping. When the man awakens from his drunken sleep, he sees that his friend has gone and so he also leaves. Unaware of the jewels in the hem of his robe, he travels from place to place trying to find work but he meets with many difficulties. And so he lives in great hardship and poverty.

Many years later, still wearing the old cloak that has become dirty and ragged, the poor man unexpectedly meets his old friend, who asks him, "How is it that you are so destitute? Long ago, before I took my leave, I sewed into the hem of your cloak many precious and valuable jewels. Have you never discovered them?" Then he took his friend's cloak and undid the stitches at the hem, revealing the precious jewels that were hidden there.

This parable is very like the parable of the destitute son, who had forgotten his true heritage as the son of a wealthy man, just as the shravakas did not know their true heritage as the children of the Buddha. The Buddha is a good friend who wants to take care of us. He has given us many precious teachings, but we remain unaware of them, we don't discover them, and so we go about our lives in great spiritual poverty. But now we can see these precious jewels that the Buddha has sewn into the hem of our cloak, and we can begin to live the life of a bodhisattva. That is the meaning of this parable offered by the 500 arhats, who through the teaching of the wonderful Dharma now see that they too, possess the capacity for Buddhahood, the true spiritual wealth of the Mahayana.

In Chapter Nine, "Prophecies Conferred on Learners and Adepts," the Buddha predicts Buddhahood for two monks, Ananda and Rahula, who serve as the representatives of all the bhikshus and bhikshunis

who are still young in the practice. The Buddha predicts their Buddhahood in order to show that not only those of advanced age and
spiritual accomplishment will attain Buddhahood but also young
monks and nuns have the capacity to become a Buddha as well. And
after the Buddha had predicted Buddhahood for Ananda and Rahula he
predicted Buddhahood for 2,000 others, both learners—those still in
training to learn how to put the teachings into practice; and adepts—
those who have completed their training, who have enough understanding and knowledge to bring the practice into every moment of
their lives.

The terms "in training" and "those who no longer train" here have
to be understood in a special way, not in the conventional way we
might understand those who study or those who do not study in the
world. Those in training (learners) have not yet mastered the practice,
while those who no longer train (adepts) have. Yet even those who have
much more to learn, who have just set out on the path, are predicted
to become a Buddha, just as adepts, arhats, and great disciples have
been. This prophecy reflects the great inclusiveness of the *Lotus Sutra*'s
teaching. No one is left out; the white ox cart of the One Vehicle is spa-
cious enough to carry everyone to Buddhahood. And in the next chapter, we will see how this spirit of inclusiveness was expanded even more
by later additions to the sutra.

❧ NINE

Devadatta

BUDDHIST SCHOLARS have determined that *Lotus Sutra* Chapters Twelve, Thirteen, and Fourteen were very late additions to the sutra in its long process of development. The content of these three chapters suggests that they were later added to further expand the sutra's affirmation of the Buddhanature of all beings. In Chapter Twelve, Buddha predicts Buddhahood for his cousin, Devadatta. This chapter aims to establish that even those who commit the five grave offenses have not lost the potential to become Buddha.[22] The Buddha uses the example of the most difficult person, someone who has committed the worst possible offense against the Buddha and Sangha, to reaffirm that *all* living beings have Buddha nature.

The story of Devadatta is well-known. He was a very bright and highly charismatic monk who, because of his ambition, brought about a schism in the Sangha. Devadatta first tried to get the Buddha to appoint him leader of the Sangha. The Buddha was then over seventy years old, near the end of his life and ministry. But while he considered himself to be a teacher and an inspiration, the Buddha didn't think of himself as the leader of the Sangha and he didn't want to appoint someone as a leader, either. So he refused Devadatta's request.

Devadatta then allied himself with Prince Ajatashatru, Bimbisara's son, and the two schemed to usurp the kingdom so that Ajatahatru could ascend the throne and Devadatta could gain control of the Sangha. Devadatta went before an assembly of the Buddha's Sangha and proposed a set of ascetic guidelines for the monks, trying to show that his way of practice was more serious and austere.[23] The Buddha did not accept these new guidelines for the Sangha but said that any monk who wished to practice them was free to do so. Devadatta was highly charismatic and he was able to persuade nearly 500 monks to join his new Sangha. Many of these monks were young and had not yet had much opportunity to learn from the Buddha.

In this way, Devadatta brought about the first schism of the Buddhist Sangha. He and his group went to live on Mount Gayashisa and Ajatashatru supported them with donations of food and medicine. Then Ajatashatru initiated his plan to take over the kingdom. After an attempt on his father's life was unsuccessful, he had his father put under house arrest and deprived him of food so that he would starve to death. Queen Vaidehi, wife of Bimbisara and Ajatashatru's mother, visited her husband every day, hiding food on her person, and for awhile she was able to keep the king nourished. But her subterfuge was discovered and Ajatashatru barred her from seeing the king. The king eventually died in confinement.

The Buddha's personal physician, Jivaka, also served Queen Vaidehi. Through Jivaka, the Buddha learned of Ajatashatru's schemes and that Devadatta was behind them. Devadatta was also behind three attempts on the Buddha's life. The first time a swordsman was sent to assassinate him. But when he saw the Buddha sitting in meditation in the moonlight he was not able to carry out the murder. Instead he knelt before the Buddha and confessed. According to the plan, once he had killed the Buddha the assassin was to leave the mountain by a certain path, unaware that he himself would be killed in order to cover up the murder. So the Buddha advised him to go down a different path and then, with his mother, flee to the neighboring kingdom of Kosala for refuge.

In the second attempt, the would-be murderers rolled a big boulder down from the mountaintop. The stone struck the Buddha, and though it did not kill him his left foot was badly wounded and he lost a lot of blood. In the third attempt, Devadatta's men released a wild elephant to attack the Buddha, but the Buddha was able to calm the animal and was not harmed. The Buddha survived all three attempts on his life and he did not leave the kingdom, even though it was a very difficult time for him. He continued to stay and practice there and through the practice he exemplified nonviolent resistance to oppression.

Eventually, with the help of the bhikshus Shariputra and Maudgalyayana, who visited Devadatta's Sangha to teach and help the young monks, nearly everyone returned to the Buddha and the schism in the Sangha was healed. Later on Devadatta became very sick and was near death. He was so weak and ill that he could not stand or walk on his own anymore, so he asked two monks to carry him to Gridhrakuta Peak. There, before the Buddha, Devadatta said, "I take refuge in the Buddha, I go back to the Buddha and take refuge in him," and the Buddha accepted him back into the Sangha.

Sometime later, Ajatashatru was also struck down, by a mental ill-ness. He was filled with remorse and afflicted in body and mind because he had killed his own father and had done many bad things in order to gain power. He consulted various teachers and healers but no one could cure him. Finally, he consulted with Jivaka, who advised him to go directly to the Buddha. Ajatashatru was ashamed. He said, "I cannot go to the Buddha. He must be very angry at me!" But Jivaka assured him, "No, the Buddha has a lot of compassion, he is not angry with you. If you go to him and ask him with all your heart, he will help you overcome this illness."

Jivaka arranged for Ajatashatru to attend a Dharma talk by the Bud-dha in the Mango Grove, at the foot of Gridhrakuta Peak. The Bud-dha spoke on the fruits of the practice, and after the talk the king was invited to ask a few questions. The Buddha took this opportunity to undo the knots within Ajatashatru and help him recover his health. That day the Buddha served as a skillful physician, a wise and patient psychotherapist, to the king, and a good relationship between them was restored. In fact, in the opening scene of the *Lotus Sutra* we learn that Ajatashatru is also in the audience, a detail that tells us the sutra was delivered toward the end of the Buddha's life, and which shows that Ajatashatru had returned to the family of the Buddha. From the stories of Devadatta and Ajatashatru we can see how great is the Bud-dha's power of inclusiveness, tolerance, and patience. Even though these two men had committed the worst possible offenses, through his love and compassion the Buddha was able to help them transform and rejoin the family of humanity.

This brief chapter of the *Lotus Sutra* does not recount the whole story of Devadatta, which would have been well-known to Buddhists of the time. Instead, the Buddha reveals how Devadatta had in a previous life, been a wise *rishi*, a seer, and the Buddha had been a king. That seer had given the teaching of the Lotus Blossom of the Wonderful Dharma to that king, thus setting him on the road to Buddhahood. Then the Buddha predicts the future Buddhahood of Devadatta.

In this chapter we also learn about an eight-year-old girl, the daughter of the naga king, who has the capacity to become a Buddha. This girl has a jewel of incalculable value, equal to the trichiliocosm (the thousand-millionfold world, the cosmos), which she offered to the Buddha. What is the meaning of this? When we have something that is very precious we say that it is as valuable as the trichiliocosm. Suppose while practicing walking meditation in the autumn we pick up a red leaf. If we are able to see the ultimate dimension of that leaf, all the phenomena of the universe that helped create it—the galaxies, the sun and moon, the clouds and rain, the rivers and soil—then quite naturally that one small leaf becomes a very precious jewel, as valuable as the trichiliocosm. And if we make that leaf an offering to the Buddha, then the merit of our offering is no less than the merit of the daughter of the naga king who offered a precious jewel to the Buddha. So we must not think that if we do not have precious jewels, or wealth, then we have nothing to offer the Buddha. A pebble or a leaf, if we are able to see its true nature, has the same value as an incalculably precious jewel. When we can see into the ultimate dimension of things in this way, we can see their true value as something infinitely precious.

After she had made her offering and the Buddha had accepted it, the girl asks the bodhisattva Wisdom Accumulation (Prajñakuta) and Shariputra, "I have just offered a precious jewel to the Buddha and immediately he accepted it. Did that not happen quickly?" They reply, "Very quickly." The girl continues, "My becoming Buddha can happen even quicker than that." Then the entire assembly gathered on Vulture Peak watches as the daughter of the naga king suddenly transforms into a boy and carries out all the practices of the bodhisattva, becomes a fully enlightened Buddha, and for the sake of all living beings in the ten directions proclaims the wonderful Dharma.[24]

This passage in the sutra offers another glimpse into the ultimate dimension. Right in that very place and in that very moment, the entire assembly was able to see a young child instantly realize the fruit of *anuttara samyak sambodhi*, highest, perfect enlightenment. This is the world of the ultimate dimension; there is nothing more to do or learn in order to be a Buddha and serve as a Buddha. Once you have arrived in the ultimate dimension it becomes possible to relax and do everything you need to do joyfully, without fear or anxiety. You recognize your innate Buddha nature and in that very moment you are already a Buddha, you are already what you want to become.

TEN

The Capacity of Buddhahood

IN *Lotus Sutra* Chapter Thirteen, "Fortitude," the Buddha's aunt and step-mother, Mahaprajapati, and his former wife, Yashodhara, who are both bhikshunis, receive the Buddha's prediction of their future Buddhahood. All the other nuns present in the assembly are overjoyed at this, because they know that they too have the capacity of Buddhahood. Then all the bodhisattvas in the assembly vow to preach the Lotus Blossom of the Wonderful Dharma to all living beings, leaving out none: "We shall go round and about and back and forth in the world-spheres of all ten directions and shall be able to cause living beings to write and copy this scripture, to accept it and keep it, to read and recite it, to explain its meaning, to put it into practice in accordance with Dharma, and to be rightly mindful of it—and all this shall be thanks to the majestic might of the Buddha."[25]

The aim of this chapter, which was added to the sutra later, is to affirm that women also can become a Buddha. In this way, later Mahayana scholars and interpreters attempted to redress some of the the attitudes of discrimination and non-inclusiveness of the sutra. *Lotus Sutra* Chapter Fourteen, "Comfortable Conduct," also a later addition, still bears traces of the deep-seated attitude of discrimination against women and others. For this reason, it is not as outstanding as other chapters in the sutra. But it offers a teaching on how to carry out the work of a bodhisattva in times when there are fewer opportunities to hear and practice the Dharma and there is a lot of suffering in the world.

In this chapter, Manjushri asks the Buddha, "World-Honored One, bodhisattvas are rare, and life is full of evil and unhappiness and there are so many ignorant living beings. How in the future will the bodhisattvas be able to deliver and protect the teachings of the Lotus Blossom of the Wonderful Dharma?" The Buddha said, "When bodhisattvas wish to teach this sutra in the future they should dwell securely in the Four Ways."

The first of the Four Ways is that the bodhisattva who wishes to offer teachings must dwell in the place of action and the place of closeness. "Dwelling in the place of action" means practicing patience and seeking harmony with others in everything that you do. If you are patient and tolerant of others then you can create peace and joy for yourself and, thanks to that, those around you will also feel peaceful and joyful. Patience is not weakness but a stance of moderation and restraint. You do not try to force people to adopt your views. "Dwelling in the place of closeness" means that practitioners do not choose to approach those who have worldly power, who practice wrong livelihood, or who have wrong intentions. This does not mean that you reject such people but you do not seek them out to try to convert them.

Bodhisattvas have to practice to clearly see the emptiness of dharmas, their true mark, in order not to be caught in the dualistic thoughts that are produced from wrong perceptions. A bodhisattva does not see the distinction "man" or "woman," and thus does not get caught in dualistic perceptions about beings' worthiness or unworthiness to receive the teachings. This section outlines how to properly uphold, maintain, protect, and teach this sutra. When you teach you should not wish to be paid or to receive offerings, you should not enter someone's house alone, you should be properly dressed when you teach women, and so on. These proscriptions are meant to protect people from potentially harmful situations, although of course they also reflect the social and cultural attitudes of the time.

The second of the Four Ways is that those who wish to teach must dwell in the practice of peace and joy. While teaching the sutra we should neither praise and hold others in renown, nor criticize anyone. The third method is that when we teach we should not feel jealousy or envy toward others, we should not despise anyone. When we offer teachings in this way, those who are listening will be able to easily receive the teachings and transform their minds.

The fourth method is that the bodhisattva who wishes to teach this sutra must give rise to a heart of great compassion for those who have not yet been able to hear the wonderful teachings of the Buddha, and generate the great aspiration (bodhichitta) for those who, upon hearing the sutra, do not understand or have faith in it. When that bodhisattva realizes highest, perfect enlightenment he or she will use skillful means to help such a person be able to absorb the teachings.

The aim of this chapter is to exalt the greatness of the *Lotus Sutra* and assure the aspiring bodhisattvas of later times that they too will be able to practice and teach this wonderful Dharma.

ॐ 11

Dharma Teacher

L*otus Sutra* Chapter Ten, "Preachers of Dharma," can be seen as the concluding chapter of the first section of the sutra, on the historical dimension. At the same time, this chapter opens the door to the ultimate dimension, which is the focus of the second half of the sutra. In this chapter, the importance of this Scripture of the Lotus Blossom of the Wonderful Dharma is revealed. The Dharma is as important as the Buddha, as worthy of our offerings and respect. The practice of recollecting the Buddha can take us to a point of deep transformation and bring about immeasurable merit, but recollecting the Dharma brings equal transformation and merit. The *Lotus Sutra*, "foremost among all sutras," is thus the Buddha himself. When we express our deep respect for the sutra, when we uphold and teach it, then we are at the same time expressing our respect for the Buddha.

The expression "Dharma preacher" (*dharmabhanaka*) in this chapter means the person who brings the teachings of the Buddha into the world and shares them with others. A Dharma teacher is an ambassador of the Buddha who carries his message, the message of the *Lotus Sutra*, to all ten directions of the world: everyone possesses Buddha nature, everyone has the capacity to realize Buddhahood and deliver beings from suffering. In this chapter, the Buddha not only affirms the capacity of Buddhahood for those who lived in his own time and could hear the teachings directly, but also for all those who are born and practice the Dharma after the lifetime of the historical Buddha, Shakyamuni.

The Buddha says to Bodhisattva Medicine King, "If after I have passed into nirvana there is a person who, having heard even one gatha or phrase of this *Lotus Sutra* and having rejoiced in it, that person shall

62

attain highest enlightenment and become a Buddha. And if there is a person who receives and upholds, reads and recites, explains, or copies in writing even one gatha of this sutra, or who looks upon it with reverence and makes various offerings, it is the same as if that person had made offerings to the Buddha and taken the great vow of the bodhisattva, and he or she too will become a Buddha."[26] Long after the Buddha has passed into nirvana, the future Buddhahood of any person who is able to hear the *Lotus Sutra*, even just one gatha or phrase of it—even just the title of the sutra—and at that moment give rise in their hearts to great satisfaction and joy, has already been affirmed.[27] We do not have to go back 2,500 years, climb Mount Gridhrakuta, and sit among the assembly of Shakyamuni Buddha in order to receive the benefit of this King of Sutras.

Here the *Lotus Sutra* opens the door of the ultimate dimension to us. The Buddha is none other than the Dharma. The true body of the Buddha is the Dharma body (dharmakaya). Through the Dharma, we can touch the Buddha right in the present moment. Whenever we show respect and make offerings to the Dharma, when we hear, practice, and teach it to others, we are at the same time showing respect to the Buddha. The Buddha is always with us, right here in the present moment. We need only receive this wonderful Dharma and put it into practice.

PART II
The Ultimate Dimension

❧ 12

The Jeweled Stupa

Lotus Sutra Chapter Eleven, "Apparition of the Jeweled Stupa," is very beautiful. It is presented in a very theatrical way with many vivid and detailed scenes in succession, each with its own meaning. This chapter opens the door of the ultimate dimension. In the chapters on the ultimate dimension, the sutra employs very poetic images to present profound ideas that could never be described in ordinary language. Its aim is to help us go beyond our conventional ideas and get in touch with the true nature of reality.

I once made the acquaintance of a man in New York. When people came to visit him he would usually offer them a soft drink. If the guest was well-known, he would write their name on a piece of paper, put it inside the empty bottle, and keep it as a souvenir. He had a large collection of bottles with names in them. These bottles were not really worth anything, but because they were connected to some famous personality my friend felt that they had a special value. Similarly, the personal effects left behind by great artists, scientists, political, or religious leaders—a walking stick, a hat—come to be regarded as valuable and meaningful in and of themselves. The value or sacredness of such an object is not due to its original nature or function but rather to a sense of the spiritual presence that has touched and infuses it.

In this chapter a similar phenomenon occurs. The place where a great teaching, such as the *Lotus Sutra*, has been given becomes a very valuable piece of earth. When the Buddha had delivered the teaching of the One Vehicle and affirmed the potential Buddhahood of all beings, music suddenly filled the air and a fine voice said, "Wonderful, Shakyamuni, you are teaching the *Lotus Sutra*, how wonderful!" The voice emanated from a huge jeweled stupa, 500 yojanas high and 250 yojanas wide, adorned with the seven precious materials, including gold, silver, pearls, and gems that rose from the earth and floated in the sky above Mount Gridhrakuta, where the assembly had gathered to hear the Dharma. This marvelous image symbolizes the appearance of the ultimate dimension in the Saha world. The realm of no birth and no death suddenly appears in the world of birth and death.

The Sangha has gathered on Vulture Peak. Their feet are on the Earth; they are in the historical dimension. They see their teacher Shakyamuni, they see they are among a great assembly of disciples. They are in the realm of reality that we normally perceive, subject to past, present, and future. Suddenly, with the appearance of the jeweled stupa, everyone has been transported from the realm of history into the ultimate nature of reality, where there is no time or space. From the world of relative phenomena we are able to touch the absolute, and this recognition brings about a powerful vibration, something like an electric shock. Those who have learned the art of mindfulness are finely tuned and are able to receive this vibration. The ultimate goal of our practice and studies is to be able to touch the true nature of reality with our mindfulness. In the beginning our mindfulness is not yet strong, but little by little it becomes more steady and solid. And as our mindfulness becomes more stable, the ultimate dimension of reality will appear more and more clearly to us, right here and now in the historical realm, the world of appearances.

Naturally, everyone on Mount Gridhrakuta is quite amazed at the appearance of the jeweled stupa. So on behalf of the assembly, Bodhisattva Great Joy in Teaching (Mahapratibhana) asked Shakyamuni, "Who is that speaking from within the stupa?" The Buddha smiled and said, "That is the Buddha Prabhutaratna (Many Jewels). When he was a bodhisattva he made the vow that at any time in the future, at any place where a Buddha appeared to teach the *Lotus Sutra*, he would present himself and utter words of praise."

Before this, the people in the assembly have known only one Buddha, Shakyamuni, in his manifestation in the historical dimension. Learning of the existence of Prabhutaratna, they wanted to see this Buddha of the ultimate dimension. They implored Shakyamuni, "Dear teacher, please use your magical power to open the door of the stupa so that we can see Prabhutaratna."

The Buddha said, "It is possible to do this if I call back all my transformation bodies."[1] Then he entered deep concentration and emitted a ray of brilliant light from his forehead that traveled throughout the ten directions and touched all his transformation bodies, calling them home to help open the door of the ultimate dimension for the assembly on Mount Gridhrakuta.

As the beam of light traveled through space, the Sangha could clearly see all the Buddha lands that were illuminated and these realms were all very well-ordered and beautifully adorned. In each realm was a Buddha—one of the Buddha's transformation bodies, "as numerous as the sands of the Ganges"—teaching the Dharma to great assemblies of disciples, bodhisattvas, and heavenly beings. When the beam of light reached them, in a flash all these transformation Buddhas returned to Vulture Peak and filled the space all around the mountain.

Until this moment, the Buddha's disciples believed the only Buddha that existed was their teacher, Shakyamuni. They hadn't yet known that the Buddha is present everywhere, in countless transformation bodies that are always teaching throughout the cosmos. If you have never seen your teacher in the ultimate dimension but only in the historical dimension, you may think that he or she is only the physical person you see before you, who, like you, exists in the realm of birth and death. But when the Buddha's transformation bodies appeared before them, the minds of his disciples began to open. They were no longer attached to the idea that *this* Buddha, Shakyamuni, whom they had known during his lifetime on Earth, was the only Buddha. They began to see that the historical Buddha is only one manifestation, and that the Buddha was actually everywhere in time and space in innumerable transformation bodies. For the first time they saw their real teacher—and their own true nature—in the ultimate dimension.

When all his transformation bodies had arrived, the Buddha simply spread his hands and the door of the jeweled stupa opened. Just like that, you arrive at the ultimate dimension from the historical dimension. The door is open. All the transformation Buddhas, the bodhisattvas, and the heavenly beings hovering in the space above Mount

Gridhrakuta could see inside the stupa very clearly. These beings were able to touch the ultimate dimension very easily, because they are no longer caught in outer appearances or dualistic concepts. But all the shravakas down below, on the mountain itself, could not yet see in. These disciples had only just begun to taste the flavor of the Mahayana, and the work of freeing themselves from attachment to the outer signs and appearances of reality had not yet been realized. They were still caught in ideas of existence and nonexistence, one and many, coming and going, and these dualistic concepts were a kind of glue that held them close to the surface of the Earth.

So once again the fourfold assembly appealed to their teacher, "Can you raise us up so that we can see inside the stupa?" Using his super-natural power Shakyamuni lifts everyone up to the level where they can look directly into the stupa and see the ultimate Buddha, Prab-hutaratna. "Lifting everyone up" here means helping them free themselves of attachment to the outer signs of reality.[2] When we read accounts of miraculous events in Mahayana sutras we need to be able to look past the mere words and fantastic images in order to receive the true message.

Then Prabhutaratna smiled and said, "Shakyamuni, it's wonderful that you are now teaching the *Lotus Sutra*." He made room on his lion throne and invited Shakyamuni to come and sit with him. This is a very beautiful and poetic way of revealing the teaching. The ultimate Buddha and the historical Buddha sit together and become one. When we know how to read the sutra in this way we can understand its deeper meaning. Imagine the ultimate Buddha Prabhutaratna sitting there, inviting the historical Buddha Shakyamuni into his jeweled stupa. The two Buddhas sitting there—are they one Buddha or different Buddhas?

In order to touch the ultimate dimension, we have to transcend con-ventional notions of same and different, coming and going, inside and outside, above and below, before and after, birth and death. The pur-pose of this chapter on the jeweled stupa is to open the door to the ulti-mate dimension and allow us to step from the world of birth and death into the world of no birth and no death. The realm of space in which the stupa appears is a new world in which we are no longer bound to the dualistic notions that govern the historical dimension. The images in this chapter are a wonderful skillful means to help us attain the eyes of wisdom that we need in order to be able to perceive the ultimate dimension.

If we look deeply into ourselves, we see that, like Shakyamuni, we also have many transformation bodies that are always active everywhere in the cosmos. At this very moment I am in my home country, helping the young monastics and laypeople. I am present in the form of books and tapes that have been brought into Vietnam so that people there can enjoy the teaching and practice. Right now I am in Vietnam, in England, in the United States, and in many other places, because my teaching has been able to go far and wide. My transformation bodies have even gone into prison to help inmates learn the art of mindfulness and the practice of walking and sitting meditation. When you have the eyes of signlessness and are not caught by mere appearance, you will be able to recognize me in my transformation bodies, in many other forms and places.[3] All of us have many transformation bodies: our actions, our contributions, our very way of being penetrate the entire cosmos.

Being able to leave behind the world of the historical dimension and enter the world of the ultimate dimension is not easy. For a long time we have been accustomed to perceiving reality only in terms of a process of history, in terms of time and space. So when we try to look into the true face of the ultimate dimension it's very difficult for us. We have to first transform our way of looking. This is why the shravakas in the assembly are first shown the innumerable, limitless transformation bodies of the Buddha, so that they can recognize the true nature of their teacher. When they have seen clearly the ultimate nature of Shakyamuni, then quite naturally they are able to perceive Prabhutaratna. And when the two Buddhas sit side by side on the lion throne, they show us that the historical dimension and the ultimate dimension are not separate. When we look with the eyes of wisdom we can enter nirvana right in samsara; we see that they are not two but one.

The Buddha says in a verse:

> *For the sake of the Buddha Path,*
> *I, in incalculable lands,*

From the beginning until now,
  Have broadly preached the scriptures,
But among them,
  This scripture is first.
If there is anyone who can hold it,
  Then he holds the Buddha body.[4]

The Buddha body is the Dharma body, the dharmakaya, ultimate reality. We cannot confine the true nature of the Buddha into the space of eighty years, into the framework of a particular country, into the small space and small time of the historical dimension. The Buddha is always present throughout the trichiliocosm in an infinite, incalculable number of transformation bodies. And just as the Buddha manifests in various forms in the historical dimension but his true body, the dharmakaya, abides in the ultimate, we too exist in the historical dimension but at the same time we have a Dharma body in the ultimate dimension. Our historical body has a beginning and an end and we experience the cycle of birth, old age, sickness, and death. But our Dharma body is indestructible. So while living in our historical body we practice being in touch with our Dharma body, because when we can touch the nature of our Dharma body—the ultimate dimension—we are no longer afraid of birth and death.

Rising Up from the Earth

In *Lotus Sutra* Chapter Fifteen, "Welling Up Out of the Earth," we begin to see the unborn and undying nature of the Buddha. From the point of view of our conventional understanding, we see reality as limited by the two barriers of time and space. But the *Lotus Sutra* reveals to us the eternal presence of the Buddha. Time and space are not separate.

After the great bodhisattvas had arrived from throughout the cosmos, they bowed to the Buddha and respectfully asked, "We would like to stay here so that in the future, when Shakyamuni has passed into nirvana, we shall be able to continue practicing and upholding the teaching of the *Lotus Sutra* and help in the work of bringing all beings in this Saha world to the other shore." The Buddha smiled and said, "Thank you very much for your goodwill, but there are enough bodhisattvas right here on Earth to take care of this Saha world." As he spoke, the ground of the Gridhrakuta mountain "trembled and split" and "an incalculable thousands of myriads of millions" of great bodhisattvas rose up from within the Earth. These bodhisattvas had bodies of pure gold and each of them had a great number of followers, as numerous as the grains of sand in the great Ganges River.

In the Upper Hamlet of Plum Village where I live there is an area where daffodils manifest in late February. When we first arrived on the land to begin building Plum Village, we were not aware that there were so many beautiful daffodils, hundreds of thousands of them, waiting there to manifest in early spring. We had only a historical perception of the land; we had not yet seen its ultimate dimension. The daffodils don't bloom any other time of the year. Then suddenly tens of thousands of them spring up, just like the bodhisattvas welling up from the Earth. When these golden flowers manifest it is very beautiful and so we have named that place "Treasure of the Dharma Body." You cannot see the the Dharma realm (dharmadhatu), until it manifests to you. If you are too attached to your perception of the historical dimension of reality, you may not be able to see the ultimate dimension manifest. When you know how to look deeply into the historical dimension, you touch the ultimate dimension.

Everyone was amazed to see so many beautiful bodhisattvas rising up from inside the Earth, all of them great bodhisattvas, very powerful and accomplished, and all of them disciples of the Buddha Shakyamuni, the teacher of this world-sphere. The Buddha's disciples, such as Shariputra and Mahamaudgalyayana, are very eager to know how Shakyamuni, who has lived only a short while on Earth, could produce so many disciples. Some, like Ashvajit and Kaundinya, have been with the Buddha right from the beginning and so they know that Shakyamuni has been teaching for only thirty-five or forty years. How can it be that he has so many bodhisattva disciples?

The people in the assembly gathered on Gridhrakuta Peak have only begun to glimpse their teacher in the ultimate dimension. They have seen his incalculable transformation bodies that simultaneously exist throughout the cosmos. But in terms of time, of life span, they still think of him as being of the historical dimension. They know him in his physical body in this lifetime, as the worldly person sitting there before them, who has taught them only for the last forty years. They have not yet seen the totality of the ultimate nature of the Buddha, in time as well as space. In fact, the Buddha's life span is limitless too, just as his manifestations in form, in space, are infinite. So Shakyamuni looks deeply into the Earth and reveals to them his timelessness in the ultimate dimension.

When the bodhisattvas from other parts of the cosmos arrived here they saw that compared to the realms they had come from, the Earth is small and there is a lot of suffering here. They saw that Shakyamuni Buddha was working very hard to relieve the suffering of beings in this Saha world, and so they offered to stay and help the Buddha. This part of the *Lotus Sutra* gives the very clear impression that our world is not as vast or beautiful as other cosmic world-spheres, that there is a lot of suffering on this small planet Earth. But the Buddha Shakyamuni is a child of the Earth and he wants to take care of it. The appearance of countless myriads of bodhisattvas welling up from the Earth shows the cosmic bodhisattvas that the Buddha has many disciples who are ready to hold the Earth tenderly in their arms and help take care of her as well. This is a skillful means of the Buddha to help his worldly disciples touch the ultimate dimension, to realize the true nature of their teacher and also to realize their own true nature. When we touch the ultimate dimension and get in touch with our true Buddha nature, we see that there is no need to feel despair. We ourselves have the capability to take care of the Earth.

This part of the *Lotus Sutra* is concerned with "appearance." In order to be able to reach the minds of human beings, who are still attached to their perception of the historical dimension of reality, the world of birth and death, coming and going, existence and nonexistence, the Buddha appeared as a historical person called Shakyamuni. He appeared to be born, to realize the path, teach the Dharma for forty years, and then to "disappear" into nirvana. But this manifestation of the Buddha was only a kind of skillful pretense to enter the world of human beings in order to help them to liberation.

One day while practicing walking meditation in the Upper Hamlet, I looked down and saw that I was about to step on a golden-yellow leaf. It was in the autumn, when the golden leaves are very beautiful. When I saw that beautiful golden leaf I did not want to step on it and so I hesitated briefly. But then I smiled and thought, "This leaf is only pretending to be gold, pretending to fall." In terms of the historical dimension, that leaf was born on a branch as a new green bud in spring, had clung to that branch for many months, changed color in autumn, and one day when a cold wind blew it fell to the ground. But looking deeply into its ultimate dimension, we can see that the leaf is only pretending to be born, to exist for a while, and to grow old and die. The teachings of interdependence and no-self reveal to us the true unborn and undying nature of all phenomena. One day that leaf will pretend to be born again on the branch of another tree, but she is really just playing a game of hide and seek with us.

We are also playing a game of hide and seek with one another. It is not only the Buddha who pretends to be born and to enter nirvana, we also pretend to be born, to live for awhile, and to pass away. You may think that your mother has passed away and is no longer here with you. But her passing away was just a pretense, and one day, when the causes and conditions are sufficient, she will reappear in one form or another. If you have enough insight you will be able to recognize your mother in her other forms. We need to look deeply into all those we love and recognize their true nature. We love our teacher, our father and mother, our children, our brothers and sisters, and when someone we love passes away we feel great sorrow and believe we have lost that person. But ultimately, nothing is lost. The true nature of those we love is unborn and undying. If we can be in touch with the ultimate dimension, we shall smile with the yellow leaf, just as we can smile at all the other changes which take place in our lives.

So with the help of their teacher, the disciples on Gridhrakuta Peak saw into their own true Buddha nature. And just as the life span of a Buddha is limitless, so too the life span of all beings is limitless in the ultimate dimension.

❧ FOURTEEN

Infinite Life

C HAPTER FIFTEEN of the *Lotus Sutra* raised the question of limitless life and Chapter Sixteen, "The Life Span of the Thus Come One" supplies the answer. This is a new style of presentation in the sutra, and it is a skillful literary device that serves to arouse the curiosity of the reader. At the end of Chapter Fifteen, after the Buddha revealed his timeless nature, there were some among the assembly who had a hard time grasping this. They asked the Buddha to explain more about how it can be that he has taught so many myriads of bodhisattva disciples, when they have seen him teach for only forty years on Earth:

> *We beg you now, on this account,*
> *With regard to these incalculable bodhisattvas,*
> *How in little time*
> *You taught and converted them, enabling them to open up their*
>   *thought.*[5]

The Buddha said to them, "My friends, you should trust and understand that the words spoken by the Tathagata are the truth.[6] When I speak I tell the truth and you must believe and understand my words." The sutra notes that the Buddha repeated this admonition three times. Because we do not hear the explanation right away, this scene serves to heighten the suspense. First, we have to trust the Buddha's teaching. A Tathagata never utters a falsehood, never says anything that is not in accord with the truth. The Buddha's word and person are in themselves a guarantee of the truth of what he teaches, but there are those among the assembly who still feel some doubt, because what the Buddha has taught is not in accord with their own perception of things.

This detail is to show us that reasoning, concepts, and our general way of observing reality through our intellect only is a limited perception, and it can be mistaken. So we should not be attached to ideas and concepts, we should not base too much on them. We may feel that what the Buddha teaches is quite unbelievable but that is because our insight is not yet very deep. If we had deeper insight into the true nature of reality, as the Buddha does, we would be able to perceive things differently. We have to generate a spirit of trust toward the teachings, be willing to let go of our notions and examine the teachings in the light of our practice of mindfulness.

Then the Buddha began to describe his limitless life span. He is not just Shakyamuni, who has taught for the last forty years on Earth; in fact he has been a Buddha for "hundreds of thousands of myriads of millions of *nayutas* of kalpas." Then he gives an example: Suppose that five hundred thousand myriads of millions of nayutas of *asamkhyeyas* of trichiliocosms were ground into dust by someone, and then that person traveled in an eastern direction.[7] Every time he passed over an equally vast number of cosmic realms, he deposited one particle of dust, continuing in this way until every grain of dust had been deposited.

Can we conceive of such vastness of time and space? Our little planet Earth, if it were ground into dust, would give us so many trillions of grains of dust. But here the Buddha is speaking of the number of grains of dust that would result from an infinite number of trichiliocosms, great chiliocosms of worlds. And after this amount is distributed in one direction, one particle of dust at a time, you travel in the other directions. You keep doing this until you have deposited all the incalculably vast numbers of particles of dust. The time required to do this is the amount of time since Shakyamuni Buddha realized Buddhahood until now.

The Buddha says, "I have been living in this Saha world for this great incalculable period of time, teaching the Dharma to innumerable living beings; and I have also been in an equally vast number of other world-spheres, teaching and helping beings." The life span of the Buddha is not only spoken of in terms of time but also of space—immeasurable, infinite dimensions of time and space that are beyond the reach of intellectual conceptualization. So our idea of the Buddha as a purely historical person who lived 2,500 years ago, who passed into nirvana and is no longer able to be present with us here and now, is merely a misperception.

Other Mahayana sutras speak of the unborn and undying nature of the Buddha. For instance, the *Vajracchedika Sutra* says, "The Tathagata comes from nowhere and goes nowhere." But in the *Lotus Sutra*, this truth is expressed in vivid images, like a beautiful painting, and it is easier to understand and grasp through such poetic imagery.

This chapter further illuminates several themes that are central to the *Lotus Sutra* teaching, such as skillful means and the concept of appearances. The Buddha says,

> When living beings come before me, I use my eye of wisdom to observe what obstacles brought about by ignorance they have, and what form of teaching would be most beneficial for them. Then I use the wisdom of skillful means in order to teach the wonderful Dharma so that all living beings can be transformed. There are living beings who like and appreciate the small vehicle, so I use skillful means to appear to be born, practice, realize enlightenment, teach the Dharma, and enter nirvana, in order to guide these practitioners onto the Buddha path and help them transform. But in fact the Tathagata has already been a Buddha, and has been teaching beings in this and many other worlds, from beginningless time.[8]

The appearance of the Buddha in the historical dimension, as a particular person born into a particular family, and having a normal human life span, is like a magic show designed to capture the attention of the living beings of that time and guide them to the path of transformation. In the chapters of the *Lotus Sutra* discussed in Part One, on the historical dimension, the Buddha used various skillful means in teaching the paths of the three vehicles, when in fact there is really only One Vehicle. We could say that of all the Buddha's methods of teaching, his appearance in the form of various historical Buddhas throughout time and space is the ultimate skillful means. Through this method, the Tathagata has never stopped teaching and guiding beings to liberation.

We sometimes use the expression "The Eight Outer Forms of Realizing the Path" to mean the appearances or forms through which every Tathagata passes: entering the womb, being born, getting in touch with suffering, becoming a practitioner, following the path, attaining enlightenment, teaching the Dharma, and entering nirvana. We practice in order to see that these outer forms of reality are really only magical appearances. In fact, the Buddha is not born and does not die; that is the true nature of the Buddha and of everything else. When we look deeply enough into any phenomenon—a pebble, a drop of dew, a leaf, a cloud—we recognize its ultimate nature in the Three Dharma Seals of impermanence, no-self, and interdependence. In this way we can discover its true nature of no birth, no death, which is exactly the same as the true nature of the Tathagata. A beautiful golden leaf in autumn is also just putting on a magical show for us. First the leaf plays at being born in the springtime, and later it pretends to fall down to earth and die. As far as the phenomenal world is concerned, we believe that the leaf comes into being and then passes away. But in terms of the ultimate dimension, birth and death, coming and going, existence and nonexistence are only a magic display, a mere appearance.

A few years ago I was asked by a journalist in Holland, "Thây, you are now over seventy. What do you want to do before you die?" From the perspective of the ultimate dimension I could not answer her question. I don't feel that there is anything I *have* to do before I die, because I don't see that I will die. Since I began the practice I enjoy everything I do, and I have always been doing everything I want to do—teaching, sharing the practice with others, helping my students build Sanghas everywhere in the world so that individuals, communities, and nations may realize the path of freedom, peace, and joy. I once wrote in a poem:

> *The work of building will take ten thousand lifetimes.*
> *But dear one, look—*
> *That work has been achieved ten thousand lives ago.*[9]

This is speaking from the point of view of the ultimate dimension. Do you need to become a Buddha? Do you need to run after enlightenment? The wave does not have to seek to become water—she *is* water, right here and now. In the same way, you are already nirvana, you are already a Buddha. You are already what you want to become. What is essential is to enter the path of practice in order to realize this truth and help others realize it too.

With his limitless life span, the Buddha has unbounded capacity to help living beings throughout space and time, in all the realms of existence. But he plays at the pretense of coming and going, being born and passing into nirvana, as a kind of skillful means to encourage living beings to enter the path of practice. To illustrate this, the Buddha uses the example of a brilliant, talented physician who was able to refine innumerable, limitless, different kinds of medicine in order to heal various kinds of disease. The doctor had many children, and one day he had to go to another country to work. While he was away his children, lacking mindfulness, drank some poisonous concoctions. All the children were in much pain; some writhed on the ground, driven to madness. When the doctor returned home he saw what was happening and immediately concocted a variety of medicines to cure his children.

Those of the physician's children whose minds and bodies were not very disturbed were able to recognize their father and have faith in him. They readily took the medicines he gave them and gradually were able to regain their health and well-being. The others were also very happy to see their father after such a long time away, but because they relied on him too much they did not take the medicine. As long as their father was present they felt well enough, and they thought they could always take the medicine later on. The doctor saw that some of his children, thinking he would be with them forever, had no motivation to take the medicine and help heal themselves.

This made him very sad. Every day he urged them to take the medicine, but the more he said this the more they refused. So the skillful physician pretended to leave again. He asked a friend to go to his house and tell his children that their father had died. Only then, weeping disconsolately, did the children take the medicine.

In terms of the ultimate dimension, the life span of the Tathagata is immeasurable and infinite. Yet even though in ultimate reality the Buddha is not born and does not die, nevertheless he pretends to be born, to exist for awhile, and to enter nirvana to show living beings of the world how to take care of themselves. The Buddha gives us the spiritual medicine we need for the healing and transformation of our bodies and minds—the practice of mindfulness. Now it is up to us to take the medicine and practice diligently so that we too can get in touch with the ultimate dimension and recognize our true nature of no birth and no death.

We have to use mindfulness in order to touch the ultimate dimension. When we notice a yellow leaf underfoot during walking meditation, it is an opportunity to be look deeply into its nature of no coming and no going. When we breathe mindfully we are in touch with our breath and body, and we already feel different from before. Using mindfulness, everything appears to us more clearly. The practice of mindfulness is the path that leads us to the ultimate dimension. When we practice mindfulness in our daily life activities—working, gardening, cooking, washing the dishes, greeting guests—we are in touch with the phenomenal world very deeply, much more deeply than when we do not have mindfulness. At that point the ultimate dimension can begin to show itself to us.

The ultimate dimension reveals itself either vaguely or clearly to us depending on the quality of our mindfulness. Sometimes we have mindfulness only for a moment; sometimes we can maintain it for two or three minutes. If we look at a cloud mindfully and are able to maintain our mindfulness for three minutes, for those three minutes we have concentration, samadhi. When our practice of mindfulness is solid and steady enough then we are able to keep the lamp of samadhi alight from moment to moment. Whether we are in the kitchen, bedroom, bathroom, or office, when we sweep the courtyard or drive our car, in all these actions we maintain the bright flame of samadhi. Practicing this way we get in touch with our own true nature, which is exactly the same as the Buddha's, unborn and undying. Just like the yellow leaf and everything else we see around us in the world of appearances, we too are participating in the infinite life span of the Buddha.

ॐ FIFTEEN

Merit

CHAPTERS SEVENTEEN, Eighteen, and Nineteen of the *Lotus Sutra* all have to do with the idea of merit. The word "merit" (Sanskrit: *punya*), when rendered in Chinese is made up of two characters. The first character means "daily practice or daily work," and the second means "virtuous conduct." Merit is a kind of spiritual energy that can be accumulated when we maintain a steady practice. This energy protects us and brings us joy and insight. Our practice helps us see, hear, and understand things clearly and we can be present in a very deep way. When we can maintain our mindfulness and deep presence, we are able to touch the ultimate dimension. And when we get in touch with the ultimate, we know we are already in nirvana. This is the merit of the practice.

Chapter Seventeen, "Discrimination of Merits," shows us the different benefits and merit that result from receiving and practicing the wonderful Dharma of the *Lotus Sutra*. In this chapter we learn that those who have the opportunity to hear the *Lotus Sutra* and while listening give rise to a feeling of joy, contentment, and faith—even if only for one thought-instant—will receive infinite merit. Hearing this sutra, receiving it in faith, and putting its teachings into practice confer such great spiritual benefit because our faith and practice plant very good seeds in our store consciousness (*alaya vijñana*).[10] Thanks to these good seeds, in the future we will be able to realize the fruit of our practice.

In Chapter Sixteen of the sutra, we learned about the infinite life span of the Tathagata. We have seen that the Tathagata is present in endless time and infinite space. When we are in contact with the Buddha of the ultimate dimension and we are able to receive that truth, understand it, and have faith in it, then we ourselves are very close to enjoying the fruit of Buddhahood. In this chapter, the Buddha relates how countless living beings in innumerable world-spheres, on hearing the Buddha teach the wonderful Dharma of the Lotus Flower, understand and have faith in the unborn, undying nature of the Buddha. They have received the merit of the ultimate truth. We, too, have been given this teaching, but our minds must be open enough to receive it and accept it. Someone whose mind is narrow, who has little faith and understanding, will not be able to contain and bear such a great truth.

Suppose you have a small balloon that can only hold a little air; if you pump too much air into it, the balloon will burst. This is like the minds of those whose insight is not yet very deep, whose faith and understanding are limited and unstable—they do not yet have the capacity to receive and accept very profound teachings. The capacity to receive is called *kshanti*, which is one of the six *paramitas*, the practices of the bodhisattva path. We will learn more about the six paramitas later in this book, but for now we can better understand kshanti as "all-embracing inclusiveness." Kshanti is often translated as "forbearance," but this implies something unpleasant that must be endured. In fact we need kshanti, inclusiveness, in order to be able to receive and hold great happiness as well. If the capacity of our heart is not yet very great, is still not strong enough, we are not able to bear great happiness. Some people, on hearing that they have won the lottery, may faint or have a heart attack because they do not yet have the capacity to endure such good news.

The teaching of the *Lotus Sutra* on the ultimate dimension is a very great, joyful truth. From our limited perspective of reality we have etched in our minds the idea of birth and death, of coming and going, existence and nonexistence. We have gotten used to this view of reality. And now someone comes along and opens up the treasure of the ultimate for us, the priceless truth of no birth, no death, of infinite life span, essential Buddha nature, and imminent Buddhahood. Are we able to bear such a profound truth or not? When we hear the Buddha teach this truth—and we are able to practice it, bear it, accept it, and hold it in our hearts, smile and have faith in it—then we will enjoy the fruit of great merit.

This chapter describes how countless bodhisattvas were able to realize the fruits of their practice through the *dharani* called "keeping what has been heard." Dharani has the meaning of a mystical incantation, a word or phrase that holds great spiritual power, like a mantra; and it also means "to be able to hold or maintain." The dharani of "keeping what has been heard" is the bodhisattva's capacity to uphold and preserve the teachings, and to practice and share with others the truths that they have been able to hear and understand. These countless great bodhisattvas have attained "the ability to speak with unobstructed eloquence," which allows them to express things in such a way that others can understand, and so they travel throughout all the world-spheres to teach and guide others to the truth.

Then the Buddha says to Bodhisattva Maitreya, "If a good man or woman should hear me teach about the infinite life span of the Tathagata and give rise to a feeling of faith and understanding, that person is already sitting in the great assembly on Mount Gridhrakuta at this very moment." This is the merit of receiving and practicing the *Lotus Sutra*. If you are able to hear this wonderful Dharma from a friend or teacher, from a bird singing or the sound of a flowing stream; if you read or hear the sutra, understand and have faith in it, get in touch with the ultimate dimension of the Tathagata and of everything in the universe, then right in that moment you are sitting alongside the Buddha. You do not have to go back 2,500 years to be able to see and touch the Buddha. You are able to realize that profound happiness right away, in this very moment.

Chapter Eighteen, "The Merits of Appropriate Joy," tells us how we can share the happiness we have received from hearing this wonderful Dharma, accepting it in faith, and putting it into practice. Some of us still harbor doubt when we hear the *Lotus Sutra*; we are not yet able to grasp it, not yet able to take in fully what is being taught. Our hearts and minds are not yet expansive enough to bear the profound joy of this teaching; we have not perfected our practice of kshanti, inclusiveness. But we have a friend who was able to hear and understand the teaching and receive the fruit of her or his practice. That person, naturally, has great joy, and when we see our friend's happiness we also begin to feel happy. This is called "joyfully sharing the merit."

So great and far-reaching is the spiritual benefit of this wonderful Dharma that you need only to give rise to one instant, one thought of joy in your heart upon encountering the teaching and you will also receive the merit.

Chapter Nineteen, "The Merits of the Dharma Preacher," explains how the one who teaches the Dharma has the responsibility of sharing with others the truth of the *Lotus Sutra*. A Dharma teacher is someone who already has great faith in the truth of the ultimate dimension. Having realized great understanding and insight, we have a lot of energy and happiness, and we then take up the path of sharing the merit of our happiness and insight with others.

"Merit" here also has the meaning of "realization." The merit of this teaching effects a great change in the field of our six sense organs (*sadayatana*)— our eyes, ears, nose, tongue, body, and mind. When we are able to receive the truth of the *Lotus Sutra* our sense perceptions undergo a profound transformation. Automatically our eyes are able to see things that before we were not able to see. We attain the eyes of Dharma that are able to look deeply and to see the true nature and suchness of all dharmas, all phenomena in the world of our perceptions. With Dharma eyes we can look into a wilted and yellow autumn leaf and see its wonderful, fresh green nature. We can see that one leaf, whether old and yellowed or green and fresh, contains all the merits, all the wonderful suchness of the universe. The eyes of someone who has received and who maintains the teaching of this sutra, the truth of the ultimate, are able to see the limitless life span, the unborn and undying nature of everything. This is the first merit, the transformation of our sight perception into the eyes of Dharma.

With the ears of Dharma, we are now able to hear very deeply. We hear the music of the birds singing, the sound of the wind in the pine trees, and even the very subtle sound of a flower opening. And while we are listening to these sounds, we experience their wondrous ultimate nature. Bird song expresses the truth of the ultimate dimension of all phenomena. Listening deeply to the sound of the wind in the pine trees, we hear the teachings of the *Lotus Sutra*. In the same way, all of our senses are transformed. When each of our sense organs comes into contact with an object, we receive the truth of the *Lotus*

Sutra, culminating in the transformation of the mind faculty (*man-aindrya*), our mental perception.

When our mind faculty and our other sense faculties have been transformed and purified as a result of the merit we have received from hearing, understanding, and practicing this wonderful Dharma, then we need hear only one gatha or one line of the sutra to understand all sutras and teachings. We do not need to study the entire Tripitaka in order to understand the Buddhadharma. One gatha contains all other gathas, one teaching reveals the deep meaning of all other teachings, just as the truth of impermanence contains the truth of no-self and the truth of interbeing. This is the meaning of the *Avatamsaka Sutra:* the one contains the all.

Having received this great merit, with our mind faculty transformed, any thought we have, any concept we entertain—all have the flavor of the Buddhadharma. Even though we may not yet have realized perfect wisdom or put an end to all our mental afflictions (*kleshas*), with a purified mind faculty every thought, every calculation, every deduction, every word we speak is in accord with the Buddhadharma. There is nothing we teach that is not the truth, and the value of what we teach is equivalent to that of the Dharma taught by all the Buddhas in the sutras. The far-reaching merit of the *Lotus Sutra* transforms all those who hear it, understand it, accept it in faith, and practice it into teachers of Dharma who share their insight and joy with others in order to help them realize the truth of the ultimate dimension and cross to the shore of freedom.

❧ SIXTEEN

The Light of Mindfulness

To complete our discussion of the ultimate dimension we skip ahead to *Lotus Sutra* Chapter Twenty-One, "The Supernatural Powers of the Thus Come One." The supernatural power, or spiritual energy, of the Tathagata is his capacity to realize the practice. Naturally this spiritual power is based in the infinite life span of the Tathagata, the Buddha's ultimate nature. We have already seen that the Tathagata cannot be placed in a frame of calculable space and time. The Tathagata is beyond our conception of the bounds of space and time. The Tathagata is not one but many; the Tathagata is not only here in this moment but everywhere at all times, in manifestation bodies as numerous as the sands of the Ganges. So, based on the foundation of his infinite life span and ultimate nature, we can see that the spiritual power of the Tathagata is very great, beyond our ability to imagine it.

The essential message of Chapter Twenty-One is that our practice is to share in the Tathagata's limitless lifespan and great spiritual power. Just as when we look deeply into a leaf, a cloud, or any phenomenon, we are able to see its infinite lifespan in the ultimate dimension, and we realize that we are the same. If we look deeply enough, we will discover our own nature of no birth, no death. Like the Buddha, we also exist and can function in a much greater capacity than the ordinary frame of time and space we perceive ourselves to be bounded by.

We participate in the Buddha's infinite life span and limitless spiritual strength when we are able to get in touch with the ultimate dimension of everything we see. When we are in touch with the Tathagata's life span and spiritual power, we are also in touch with our own ultimate nature and spiritual power. Many of us go around all the time

88

feeling that we are as small as a grain of sand. We may feel that our one small human life does not have very much meaning. We struggle to get through life and at the end of our life we feel that we have accomplished very little. This is a kind of inferiority complex many people suffer from. If we see reality only in terms of the historical dimension, it may seem to us as if there is little one ordinary human being can do. But if we get in touch with the ultimate dimension of reality, we know that we are just like the Buddha. We share in the Buddha's nature—we *are* Buddha nature. When we are able to see beyond the limitations of perceived time and space, beyond our own notions of inferiority and powerlessness, we find we have great stores of spiritual energy to share with the world.

Now the Buddha realizes a very important miracle. He stretches out his tongue and his "long, broad tongue" is able to encompass the trichiliocosm. Then from each pore of his body he sends out innumerable rays of light of every color, which illuminate all the world-spheres in the ten directions. In all these realms can be seen a Buddha sitting on a lion throne under the bodhi tree, very dignified and beautiful. Each Buddha also puts out his tongue and emanates countless rays of light in the same way. As the Buddha's light reaches them, all the innumerable Buddhas in turn illuminate all the world-spheres throughout the incalculable trichiliocosm.

This passage contains very wonderful images, the kind of vivid descriptions for which the *Lotus Sutra* is well-known. First there is the beautiful image of the long, broad long tongue of the Buddha.[11] This idea does not originate in Buddhism; it existed in other spiritual traditions in India that predated Buddhism. The meaning of the image is that someone who speaks the truth is said to have a large tongue. The Buddha only speaks the ultimate truth (*paramarthasatya*), and so he is described as having a tongue so large it can cover the trichiliocosm. With his purified senses the Buddha is able to perceive very wonderful things, but when he speaks about such marvelous phenomena, people often do not believe it because they are not able to perceive in this way. So the Buddha has to remind his listeners, "I am telling you the truth. What I speak is the truth and only the truth."

Then there is the image of the rays of light emitted by the Buddha.

"Light" in Buddhist sutras is a metaphor for awakened understanding. The world of the *Avatamsaka Sutra* is a world of light. The Buddha is light; beams of light stream out from each pore of his body. His light of mindfulness is very strong, and with that source of light the Tathagata is able to illuminate all the world-spheres, as if by shining the beam of a powerful lamp into them. With the light of his great spiritual power the Buddha can see clearly whatever phenomenon the light of his mindfulness rests upon.

We also have the source of this light in our own consciousness. When we develop our capacity for mindfulness and allow it to shine within us and around us, we are able to see many things that cannot be seen in ordinary perception. When the light of mindfulness, of awakened understanding, illuminates a leaf, a blade of grass, or a cloud, we are able to see all the wonders of that phenomenon and the multidimensional world of the *Avatamsaka Sutra* is opened up to us in an amazing way. And just like the Buddha, thanks to mindfulness we too can perform miracles.

Suppose there is someone who lives very mindfully, dwelling in concentration. She comes home, goes out, stands, sits, speaks, chops vegetables, washes pots, carries out all the activities of daily life in mindfulness and concentration. In all her actions of body, speech, and mind she shines the light of mindfulness. When others encounter her they are able to get in touch with that mindfulness, and they are influenced by it. Touched by the light of her mindfulness, the seed of mindfulness in their own consciousness begins to sprout, and naturally they also begin to cultivate mindfulness in their activities as she does. This is a true miracle that any one of us can realize.

The light of mindfulness of those around us—a brother or sister, parent or teacher, spouse or partner—shines out onto us, and thanks to that we also begin to cultivate mindfulness and shine it out toward others. What is a Buddha? A Buddha is nothing other than the light of mindfulness, and that light, wherever it shines, is able to show us the wonderful truth, the ultimate dimension of whatever it illuminates. Those who are touched by the light of mindfulness in turn shine the light of their mindfulness upon other people and objects. Just as the Buddha's rays of light, when they reached all the other world-spheres, caused the countless Buddhas to emit their light, when we live mindfully we shine that light broadly all around us and help others get in touch with and shine their light of mindfulness as well.

There is a story from the Vietnamese tradition about Master Phap Tang, of the Duong era, who was teaching the *Avatamsaka Sutra* to Queen Vu Tac Thien. He had an octagonal tower built, and instructed that the interior walls of the tower be covered with large mirrors. When the tower was completed he invited the queen to enter it with him, holding a candle he had lit for her. When the queen stepped inside she saw the image of the flame reflected in the mirror in front of her. When she turned around she saw the flame reflected in the mirror behind her. But not only was the image of the candle reflected in each of the eight mirror walls—there were countless reflections of the flame, because each reflection was again reflected in all of the other mirrors, and then reflected back again and again. This was a very skillful way for Master Phap Tang to illustrate to the queen the image in the *Avatamsaka Sutra* of Indra's Net, in which each jewel suspended in the great cosmic net reflects the image of all the other jewels, creating infinite reflections of light.

This chapter, contains the image of layers and layers of causes and conditions that is also found in the *Avatamsaka Sutra*. When we live in mindfulness, it is as if there are rays of light coming from the pores of our body that touch all those around us. Then, even if someone does not yet have the practice, when they get in touch with the light of our mindfulness they begin to give rise to the seed of mindfulness within themselves. This is a natural process, and it does not require a lot of striving or effort on our part. A beam of light does not have to work hard to illuminate the objects it touches; it simply abides in its nature of illumination. Just so, we do not have to expend a lot of effort to shine the light of our mindfulness, we just continue our practice of mindfulness and naturally it will have an effect on our environment and the people around us and, in turn, they will begin to shine the light of mindfulness as well.

When we look at this in the light of the teachings of the layers of causes and conditions, we can see how even one life, one person's actions, can have a very great effect. We can no longer hold onto the idea that our one small, ordinary life doesn't matter. Our way of being has an effect on our situation, our environment, and the lives of all those around us. Just like the Buddha, we have the capacity to affect many beings and lives. When we light the lamp of mindfulness within ourselves and let it shine, everyone around us will also benefit. In Sangha life, if even one person has mindfulness, the light of that mindfulness benefits the entire community. One person gives rise to mindfulness, and then the light of that mindfulness touches another person, and their mindfulness illuminates another, and so on until every person, every jewel in the net, is shining with the light of mindfulness. In this way we can create a world of light right here on Earth.

❧ SEVENTEEN

Trust and Faith

In Chapter Twenty-Two, "Entrusting," the Buddha puts out his hand which is like heavenly silk and simultaneously strokes the heads of all the countless great bodhisattvas who have gathered to hear him teach the *Lotus Sutra*. He says to them, "For incalculable hundreds of thousands of myriads of millions of asamkhyeya kalpas I practiced and cultivated the Dharma of anuttara samyak sambodhi, so hard to obtain.[12] Now I entrust it to all of you. You must single-mindedly propagate this Dharma broadly, causing others to benefit from it." Entrusting means to commend, to leave an inheritance, to delegate to someone the responsibility of taking care of, preserving, protecting, and continuing something of great value. Here we see the Buddha conferring on all the bodhisattvas, the responsibility of preserving and teaching the wonderful Dharma of the Lotus Blossom to all living beings in the innumerable world-spheres throughout time and space.

The Buddha then gives thanks to all his emanation bodies, who have gathered from infinite numberless worlds to open the door of the jeweled stupa of Prabhutaratna. He thanks them for responding to his call and appearing in the skies above Mount Gridhrakuta, combining their spiritual strength so that the door of the stupa could be opened and the fourfold assembly on the ground below would be able to look into the ultimate dimension. This was an act of great compassion toward the assembly of shravakas, because of course the Buddhas and bodhisattvas do not need to open the stupa of Prabhutaratna in order to see the ultimate dimension. But because the Sangha wanted to see the ultimate Buddha, Shakyamuni Buddha, their teacher in the historical

93

dimension, calls all his manifestation bodies back to help him open the door to the ultimate dimension.

When all these emanation bodies came together it was a very joyful time. They drank tea together, ate biscuits, and had a dharma discussion. Then the Buddha entrusts the wonderful Dharma to the great bodhisattvas and asks them to return to all their world-spheres to continue the work of leading all beings to liberation. In this way, the sutra says, they can repay the great kindness and compassion the Buddhas have shown by teaching the wonderful Lotus Dharma. This is the true meaning of entrusting. "This teaching is the highest of all teachings. I am now handing it on to you so that you may receive it and teach it widely to benefit all living beings."

We should not think that it is only the Buddha who has so many manifestation bodies. If we look deeply we will also see that we have many emanation bodies as well. In the 1960s, I wrote a book called *The Miracle of Mindfulness* to help people learn the practice of mindfulness.[13] In writing the book I drew upon the *Satipatthana Sutta*. But it is a simple book, very practical and easy to understand. I wrote it in the form of a letter to the workers of the School of Youth for Social Service, a community of young people we had established in Vietnam to help rebuild communities that were destroyed by the war. The book was intended to help our students practice mindfulness as they went about the difficult and sometimes dangerous work of relieving the suffering of the Vietnamese people. I saw that the practice of mindfulness would be very useful in this kind of situation. If our students were able to maintain mindfulness, to breathe and smile and keep a fresh outlook when bringing relief to others, their practice of mindfulness would at the same time nourish their hearts of loving-kindness and compassion so that they could continue to do such difficult work. If they worked under too much stress and difficulty all the time and were not able to maintain mindfulness, if they became angry or resentful, or began to feel sorry for themselves, they would not be able to achieve anything in their work. So I wrote *The Miracle of Mindfulness* to help these students.

At the time I wrote that small book, I could not have imagined the effect it would have in the world. It has been translated into twenty-five languages, reprinted many times, distributed in countries throughout the world, and I still receive letters from people who have experienced tremendous transformations in their lives and work from reading this simple book and learning the practice of mindfulness. This shows that we are not able to measure or anticipate the full effect over time of the work we do. Our works, our actions, our very way of being are our emanation bodies that travel through the world widely and continue to have an effect on others for a long time.

Every one of us has many emanation bodies in all parts of the world but the result of these emanation bodies is not something we can easily measure. If we, like Buddha Shakyamuni, were to realize the miracle of gathering together all our manifestation bodies in an instant in one place, we would feel such great happiness, joy of a kind that we rarely experience. So we need to remember that our studies and practice are not only for our individual benefit but also benefit our family, community, nation, and the entire Earth. Our mistakes cause others to suffer, and our success in the practice can benefit many others. This is why it is so important to practice the art of mindfulness, so that our emanation bodies offer only love and compassion and bring benefit, not harm, to others.

The Buddha shows great faith in us by entrusting the wonderful Dharma to us. We can repay this trust and faith by becoming the arms and hands of the Buddha and continuing the Tathagata's great work of leading all beings to the shore of liberation.

PART III

The Action Dimension

❦ EIGHTEEN

Never Disparaging

ONE OF THE MOST IMPORTANT and influential schools of Chinese Buddhism, the T'ien-t'ai school, divides the *Lotus Sutra* into two parts, the first fourteen chapters representing the historical dimension and the last fourteen chapters representing the ultimate dimension. But this method has some shortcomings. There are elements of the ultimate dimension in the first fourteen chapters and elements of the historical in the second. There is also a third very important dimension, the dimension of action.

These dimensions can not be separated; they inter-are. Here is an example. When we look at a bell we can see that it is made of metal. The manifestation of the bell carries the substance of metal within. So within the historical dimension—the form of the bell—we can see its ultimate dimension, the ground from which it manifests. When the bell is struck it creates a pleasant sound. The pleasant sound created by the bell is its function. The purpose of a bell is to offer sound in order for us to practice. That is its action. Function is the dimension of action, the third dimension along with, and inseparable from, the historical and ultimate dimensions.

We need to establish a third dimension of the *Lotus Sutra* to reveal its function, its action. How can we help people of the historical dimension get in touch with their ultimate nature so that they can live joyfully in peace and freedom? How can we help those who suffer open the door of the ultimate dimension so that the suffering brought about by fear, despair, and anxiety can be alleviated? I have gathered all the chapters on the great bodhisattvas into this third action dimension, the bodhisattva's sphere of engaged practice.

Practicing the path and liberating beings from suffering is the action of the bodhisattvas. The *Lotus Sutra* introduces us to a number of great bodhisattvas, such as Sadaparibhuta (Never Disparaging), Bhaisajyaraja (Medicine King), Gadgadasvara (Wonderful Sound), Avalokiteshvara (Hearer of the Sounds of the World), and Samantabhadra (Universally Worthy). The action taken up by these bodhisattvas is to help living beings in the historical dimension recognize that they are manifestations from the ground of the ultimate. Without this kind of revelation we cannot see our true nature. Following the bodhisattva path, we recognize the ground of our being, our essential nature, in the ultimate dimension of no birth and no death. This is the realm of nirvana—complete liberation, freedom, peace, and joy.

In Chapter Twenty of the *Lotus Sutra*, we are introduced to a beautiful bodhisattva called Sadaparibhuta, "Never Disparaging." The name of this bodhisattva can also be translated as "Never Despising." This bodhisattva never underestimates living beings or doubts their capacity for Buddhahood. His message is, "I know you possess Buddha nature and you have the capacity to become a Buddha," and this is exactly the message of the *Lotus Sutra*—you are already a Buddha in the ultimate dimension, and you can become a Buddha in the historical dimension. Buddha nature, the nature of enlightenment and love, is already within you; all you need do is get in touch with it and manifest it. Never Disparaging Bodhisattva is there to remind us of the essence of our true nature.

This bodhisattva removes the feelings of worthlessness and low self-esteem in people. "How can I become a Buddha? How can I attain enlightenment? There is nothing in me except suffering, and I don't know how to get free of my own suffering, much less help others. I am worthless." Many people have these kinds of feelings, and they suffer more because of them. Never Disparaging Bodhisattva works to encourage and empower people who feel this way, to remind them that they too have Buddha nature, they too are a wonder of life, and they too can achieve what a Buddha achieves. This is a great message of hope and confidence. This is the practice of a bodhisattva in the action dimension.

Sadaparibhuta was actually Shakyamuni in one of his former lives, appearing as a bodhisattva in the world to perfect his practice of the

Dharma. But this bodhisattva did not chant the sutras or practice in the usual way—he did not perform prostrations, or go on pilgrimages, or spend long hours in sitting meditation. Never Disparaging Bodhisattva had a specialty. Whenever he met someone he would address them very respectfully, saying, "You are someone of great value. You are a future Buddha. I see this potential in you."

There are passages in the *Lotus Sutra* that suggest that his message was not always well-received. Because they have not yet gotten in touch with the ultimate dimension, many people could not believe what the bodhisattva was telling them about their inherent Buddha nature, and they thought he was mocking them. Often he was ridiculed, shouted at, and driven away. But even when people did not believe him and drove him away with insults and beatings, Sadaparibhuta did not become angry or abandon them. Standing at a distance he continued to shout out the truth:

> *I do not hold you in contempt!*
> *You are all treading the Path,*
> *And shall all become Buddhas!*[1]

Sadaparibhuta is very sincere and has great equanimity. He never gives up on us. The meaning of his life, the fruition of his practice, is to bring this message of confidence and hope to everyone. This is the action of this great bodhisattva. We have to learn and practice this action if we want to follow the path of the bodhisattvas.

The sutra tells us that when Sadaparibhuta was near the end of his life he suddenly heard the voice of a Buddha called King of Imposing Sound (Bhishmagarjitasvararaja) teaching the *Lotus Sutra*. He could not see that Buddha but he clearly heard his voice delivering the sutra, and through the power of the teaching, Never Despising Bodhisattva suddenly found that his six sense organs were completely purified and he was no longer on the verge of death. Understanding deeply the message of the *Lotus Sutra*, he was able to touch his ultimate dimension and attain deathlessness.

We have already learned about the infinite life span of a Buddha in the ultimate dimension. In terms of the historical dimension, a Buddha may live 100 years or a little bit more or less; but in terms of the ultimate dimension a Buddha's life span is limitless. Sadaparibhuta saw that his lifespan is infinite, just like the life span of a Buddha. He saw that every leaf, every pebble, every flower, every cloud has an infinite life span also, because he was able to touch the ultimate dimension in everything. This is one of the essential aspects of the *Lotus* message. When his sense organs had been purified, he could see very deeply and understand how the six sense organs (eyes, ears, nose, tongue, body, and mind) produce the six kinds of consciousness. When his senses had been purified he was capable of touching reality as it is, the ultimate dimension. There was no more confusion, no more delusion, in his perception of things.

This passage describes a kind of transformation that we too can experience. When the ground of our consciousness is prepared, when our sense consciousnesses and our mind consciousness have been purified through the practice of mindfulness and looking deeply into the ultimate nature of reality, we can hear in the sound of the wind in the trees or in the singing of the birds the truth of the *Lotus Sutra*. While lying on the grass or walking in meditation in the garden we can get in touch with the truth of the Dharma that is all around us all the time. We know that we are practicing the *Lotus* samadhi and our eyes, ears, nose, tongue, body, and mind are automatically transformed and purified.

Having realized the truth of the ultimate, Bodhisattva Sadaparibhuta continued to live for many millions of years, delivering his message of hope and confidence to countless beings. So we can see that the *Lotus Sutra* is a kind of medicine for long life. When we take this medicine we are able to live a very long time in order to be able to preserve and transmit the teachings in the *Lotus Sutra* to many others. We know that our true nature is unborn and undying, so we no longer fear death. Just like Sadaparibhuta, we always dare to share the wonderful Dharma with all living beings. And all those who thought the bodhisattva was only making fun of them finally began to understand. Looking at Sadaparibhuta they were able to see the result of his practice, and so they began to have faith in it and to get in touch with their own ultimate nature.

This is the practice of this great bodhisattva—to regard others with a compassionate and wise gaze and hold up to them the insight of their ultimate nature, so that they can see themselves reflected there. Many people have the idea that they are not good at anything, they are not able to be as successful as other people. They cannot be happy; they envy the accomplishments and social standing of others while regarding themselves as failures if they do not have the same level of worldly success. We have to try to help those who feel this way. Following the practice of Sadaparibhuta we must come to them and say, "You should not have an inferiority complex. I see in you some very good seeds that can be developed and make you into a great being. If you look more deeply within and get in touch with those wholesome seeds in you, you will be able to overcome your feelings of unworthiness and manifest your true nature."

The Chinese teacher Master Guishan writes:

> We should not look down on ourselves.
> We should not see ourselves as worthless and always withdraw into
> the background.[2]

These words are designed to wake us up. In modern society, psychotherapists report that many people suffer from low self-esteem. They feel that they are worthless and have nothing to offer, and many of them sink into depression and can no longer function well, take care of themselves or their families. Therapists, healers, caregivers, teachers, religious leaders, and those who are close to someone who suffers in this way all have the duty to help them see their true nature more clearly so that they can free themselves from the delusion that they are worthless. If we know friends or family members who see themselves as worthless, powerless, and incapable of doing anything good or meaningful, and this negative self-image has taken away all their happiness, we have to try to help our friend, our sister or brother, our parent, spouse, or partner remove this complex. This is the action of the bodhisattva Never Disparaging.

We also have to practice so as not to add to others' feelings of worthlessness. In our daily life when we become impatient or irritated we might say things that are harsh, judgmental, and critical, especially in regard to our children. When they are under a great deal of pressure, working very hard to support and care for their family, parents frequently make the mistake of uttering unkind, punitive, or blaming words in moments of stress or irritation. The ground of a child's consciousness is still very young, still very fresh, so when we sow such negative seeds in our children we are destroying their capacity to be happy. So parents and teachers, siblings, and friends all have to be very careful and practice mindfulness in order to avoid sowing negative seeds in the minds of our children, family members, friends, and students.

When our students or loved ones have feelings of low self-esteem we have to find a way to help them transform those feelings so that they can live with greater freedom, peace, and joy. We have to practice just like Never Disparaging Bodhisattva, who did not give up on people or lose patience with them but continued always to hold up to others a mirror of their true Buddha nature.

I always try to practice this kind of action. One day there were two young brothers who came to spend the day with me. I took them both to show them a new manual printing press I had just gotten. The younger boy was very interested in the machine, and while he was playing with it the motor burned out. As I was pressing one button to show the boys how it worked, the little boy pressed another at the same time, and it overstressed the machine's engine. The elder brother said angrily, "Thây, you just wanted to show us the machine. Why did he have to do that? He wrecks whatever he touches." These were very harsh words from such a young boy. Perhaps he had been influenced by hearing his parents or other family members use blaming language like this, so he was just repeating what he had heard without realizing the effect on his little brother.

In order to help mitigate the possible effects of this criticism on the younger boy, I showed the boys another machine, a paper cutting machine, and this time I instructed the younger one how to use it. His brother warned me, "Thây, don't let him touch it, he'll destroy this one too." Seeing that this was a moment when I could help both boys, I said to the older brother, "Don't worry, I have faith in him. He is intelligent. We shouldn't think otherwise." Then I said to the younger boy, "Here, this is how it works—just push this button. Once you have released this button then you press that button. Do this very carefully and the machine will work properly." The younger brother followed my instructions and operated the machine without harming it. He was very happy, and so was his older brother. And I was happy along with them.

Following the example of Sadaparibhuta Bodhisattva, I only needed three or four minutes to remove the complex of the younger brother and teach the older brother to learn to trust in the best of his younger brother and not just see him in terms of his mistakes. In truth, at that moment I was a bit concerned that the young boy would ruin the other machine. But if I had hesitated and not allowed him to try and follow my instructions, believing that he would destroy the machine, I could well have destroyed that little boy. Preserving the health and well-being of the mind of a child is much more important than preserving a machine.

You only need to have faith in the action of Sadaparibhuta and very quickly you can help others overcome their negative self-image. Never Despising Bodhisattva shows everyone that they have the capacity for perfection within themselves, the capacity to become a Buddha, a fully enlightened one. The message of the *Lotus Sutra* is that everyone can and *will* become a Buddha. Sadaparibhuta is the ambassador of the Buddha and of the *Lotus Sutra*, and sometimes ambassadors are reviled or attacked. Sadaparibhuta was also treated this way. He brought his message to everyone, but not everyone was happy to hear it because they could not believe in their own Buddha nature. So when they heard his message they felt they were being scorned or mocked. "Throughout the passage of many years, he was constantly subjected to abuse… some in the multitude would beat him with sticks and staves, with tiles and stones."[3] The mission of a Dharma teacher, of a bodhisattva, requires a great deal of love, equanimity, and inclusiveness.

Sadaparibhuta represents the action of inclusiveness, kshanti. Kshanti, one of the six paramitas, is discussed in detail in the last section of this book. Kshanti is also translated as "patience," and we can see this great quality in Sadaparibhuta and in one of Shakyamuni's disciples, Purna, who is praised by the Buddha in the eighth chapter of the *Lotus Sutra*. While the *Lotus Sutra* only mentions Purna in passing, he is the subject of another sutra, the *Teaching Given to Maitrayaniputra*. In this sutra, after the Buddha had instructed Purna in the practice, he asked him, "Where will you go to share the Dharma and form a Sangha?" The monk said that he wanted to return to his native region, to the island of Sunaparanta in the Eastern Sea.

The Buddha said, "Bhikshu, that is a very difficult place. People there are very rough and violent. Do you think you have the capacity to go there to teach and help?"

"Yes, I think so, my Lord," replied Purna.

"What if they shout at you and insult you?"

Purna said, "If they only shout at me and insult me I think they are kind enough, because at least they aren't throwing rocks or rotten vegetables at me. But even if they did, my Lord, I would still think that they are kind enough, because at least they are not using sticks to hit me."

The Buddha continued, "And if they beat you with sticks?"

"I think they are still kind enough, since they are not using knives and swords to kill me."

"And if they want to take your life? It's possible that they would want to destroy you because you will be bringing a new kind of teaching, and they won't understand at first and may be very suspicious and hostile," the Buddha warned.

Purna replied, "Well, in that case I am ready to die. Because my dying will also be a kind of teaching and because I know that this body is not the only manifestation I have. I can manifest myself in many kinds of bodies. I don't mind if they kill me, I don't mind becoming the victim of their violence, because I believe that I can help them."

The Buddha said, "Very good, my friend. I think that you are ready to go and help there."

So Purna went to that land and he was able to gather a lay Sangha of 500 people practicing the mindfulness trainings, and also to establish a monastic community of around 500 practitioners. He was successful in his attempt to teach and transform the violent ways of the people in that country. Purna exemplifies the practice of kshanti, inclusiveness.

Sadaparibhuta may have been a future or a former life of Purna. We are the same. If we know how to practice inclusiveness then we will also be the future life of this great bodhisattva. We know that Sadaparibhuta's life span is infinite, and so we can be in touch with his action and aspiration at any moment. And when we follow the practice of inclusiveness of Never Despising Bodhisattva, he is reborn in us right in that very moment. We get in touch with the great faith and insight that everyone is a Buddha, the insight that is the very marrow of the *Lotus Sutra*. Then we can take up the career of the bodhisattva, carrying within our heart the deep confidence we have gained from this insight and sharing that confidence and insight with others.

Therapists and others in the healing professions, Dharma teachers, schoolteachers, parents, family members, colleagues, and friends can all learn to practice like Sadaparibhuta. Following the path of faith, confidence, and inclusiveness we can help free many people from the suffering of negative self-image, help them recognize their true Buddha nature, and lead them into the ultimate dimension.

NINETEEN

Medicine King

Lotus Sutra Chapter Twenty-Three, "The Former Affairs of the Bodhisattva Medicine King," introduces us to another great bodhisattva, Bhaishajyaraja, Medicine King. Just like Sadaparibhuta, this bodhisattva is also a model of enlightened action. Medicine King realizes the teachings of the *Lotus Sutra* in another sphere of action, the sphere of devotion, faith, and gratitude. Without faith it is not possible for human beings to live. Without love we cannot truly realize our full humanity. We practice the Dharma not only to gain knowledge but to transform ourselves into someone who is capable of love, affection, and gratitude. Medicine King represents this aspect. Just as Bodhisattva Sadaparibhuta has a specific role to play as the hands and arms of the Buddha, Medicine King Bodhisattva has another role to play.

In the opening scene of this chapter, one of the bodhisattvas from another part of the cosmos, Beflowered by the King of Constellations, asks the Buddha, "World-Honored One, how does the bodhisattva Medicine King travel in the Saha world?" In the Vietnamese-Chinese version of the sutra, this passage reads *du thu ta ba the gioi*, "What is his business in the Saha world?" But it is not really a matter of doing business; a better understanding of this passage would be, "How is that bodhisattva enjoying his journey in the world?" In the chapter on Avalokiteshvara in the Vietnamese version of the *Lotus Sutra* we see the phrases "enjoying a trip" and "enjoying a stay." So the great bodhisattvas are those who know how to be at ease and enjoy their travels in the Saha world.

We have to learn how to enjoy ourselves as we journey through this saha world. When we understand this, we will be more at ease and not think of our life as being some kind of task that we must accomplish. We do not have to scheme or hurry. We will be able to offer our service and work because we enjoy it. We can work without attachment to outcome. We can perform all our actions—organizing a retreat, building a Sangha, working with prisoners—in a spirit of freedom, liberation, and joy, rather than being bound up by notions of achieving a certain level of success or attainment.

Suppose someone wants to build a temple—they take measurements and draw up plans, estimate the cost of labor and materials, choose the color of the tiles, and so on, but they do all this with a feeling of contentment and ease, like someone enjoying a holiday. Without this spirit of liberation, even the Buddhas and bodhisattvas will not be able to enjoy their time in the Saha world.

The *Sutra of Forty-Two Sections*, the earliest sutra to be translated into Chinese, in the second century C.E., has the line, "The Dharma I offer is the practice of non-practice, the action of non-action."[4] We think of action and non-action as two different things. When we say, "Don't just sit there, do something!" we are urging people to act. But if someone is in a poor state of being, if they don't have enough peace, enough understanding, enough inclusiveness, if they still have a lot of anger and fear, then not only will their action have no value, it may even be harmful. The quality of our action depends on the quality of our being: skillful action arises from the foundation of being, and being is non-action. So the calm, mindful, fully present quality of our being, the quality of our non-action, is already a kind of "action" in this sense.

There are those among us who may not seem to do very much but their presence is very crucial for the well-being of their immediate situation and of the world. Maybe there is one person in a family who is not busy all the time, who does not make a lot of money, yet their absence would cause a lot of trouble in the family, because that person contributes non-action, the quality of their being. Imagine a boatload of refugees caught in a storm at sea. If everyone panics they will jump up and move around hurriedly and fearfully, further destabilizing the boat and perhaps causing it to capsize. But if there is just one person who remains calm, who with his equanimity can say, "Dear friends, stay where you are and sit quietly," that person can save the whole group.

Though he doesn't "do" anything but stay calm and help others regain their calmness, in this way catastrophe is averted. This is skillful non-action, the quality of being that is the ground of all good action.

We have to look into every action in order to see the ground of that action, the quality of being that it arises from. Sometimes you may not "do" anything yet you are doing a lot. Sometimes you do a lot. You may be always very busy attending to so many things, but you don't really accomplish much because your activities come from a place of striving that leaves you drained and incapable of experiencing the peace and joy of the present moment. There are those who even approach Buddhist practice this way—they practice very hard, meditating twelve hours a day, reciting the sutras, evoking the name of the Buddha, yet they are not transformed at all. Their anger, frustration, and resentment are still there.

"My Dharma is to take up the action of non-action, to practice the practice of non-practice, to attain the attainment of non-attainment. " This line from the sutra Sutra in 42 Chapters communicates to us that we should not be caught in the outer form, we should not discriminate between non-action and action, being and acting. Many of us try to do many things, yet the more we act the more troubled our family, society, and world become, because the foundation of our being is not yet stable enough. Try practicing the opposite: don't do anything, don't take any action right away, but improve your quality of being through meditation and mindfulness practice. To be in the here and now, fully alive, fully present, is a very positive contribution to any situation. Increasing our insight, compassion, and understanding through the practice of mindfulness is the best thing we can offer to the world. This is the practice of non-practice, the attainment of non-attainment, the action of non-action. We improve the quality of our being so that we have peace and joy, and then we can offer it to our families and communities, and to the world.

The chapter on Bhaisajyaraja in the *Lotus Sutra* tells of his past lives, of how he came to be Medicine King Bodhisattva. Formerly he studied and practiced under a Buddha called Pure and Bright Excellence of Sun and Moon (Candrasuryavimalaprabhashri), and in that time he was called Seen with Joy by All Living Beings (Sarvasattvapriyadarshana). From time to time we meet someone like this, a person whom everyone—children and adults, men and women—is glad to see. The presence of that person is so wonderful, so fresh and pleasant, that everyone is happy to see her or him.

Bodhisattva Seen with Joy by All Living Beings became a very good disciple of the Buddha Pure and Bright Excellence of Sun and Moon. He felt great devotion and love toward his teacher and the bond between them was very deep. Because of the great affection between teacher and disciple, he made a lot of progress. Looking deeply into the nature of this bodhisattva's practice we can see the devotion, dedication, love, and faithfulness.

You might wonder how devotion and affection are part of the practice of looking deeply and attaining enlightenment. Do we need to love our teacher? Do we need to love our disciples? Do we need to love our Dharma brothers and sisters in order to succeed in our practice? The answer is, yes. Just as the loving presence of the parents is quite crucial for the growth of a baby, the loving presence of a teacher is very important for his or her disciples. The loving presence of our brothers and sisters in the Sangha is very important for us to grow as practitioners. That is the message sent forth by this bodhisattva. We need love and affection, warmth and nurturance in order to grow and progress on the path.

Seen with Joy by All Living Beings progressed well in his spiritual practice and was able to realize the freedom and insight of the ultimate dimension and attain the "samadhi that displays all manner of physical bodies." He no longer identified his physical body as himself and could manifest various emanation bodies in order to help many kinds of people—if he needed to manifest as a child he became a child, if he needed to become a woman he took female form. If he needed to be a businessman he could manifest as a businessman. He always appeared in the most appropriate form for the situation, which allowed him to bring about a feeling of joy for the people he encountered. He was not caught by the idea that the body is a fixed, permanent self. He was able to manifest himself in many transformation bodies, just as the Buddha and Avalokiteshvara do, in order to help various kinds of living beings.

When the bodhisattva realized his capacity to appear in all different kinds of emanation bodies, his feeling of love for and gratitude to his teacher grew even stronger. So out of his great love and gratitude, and with the profound insight into his ultimate nature, he was able to relinquish his body very easily. The sutra tells us that as an offering to the Buddha and to display his insight that the body is not a permanent, unchanging self, he poured fragrant oil on himself and allowed himself to be burned by fire. This is a quite radical demonstration of his freedom and insight, one that was made out of a very deep love.

Many people know about the Vietnamese monks who immolated themselves in the 1960s. This practice has its roots in this chapter of the *Lotus Sutra*.[5] Because they had realized the insight into their ultimate nature and were no longer attached to an idea of the physical body as the self, the monks were free to use their bodies to deliver a powerful message. They transformed their bodies into torches to illuminate the suffering of the Vietnamese people. Only those who are truly free, who have seen deeply into the ultimate dimension, can make this kind of action. When you realize that your present physical form is not a permanent and fixed entity, that you can and will take many forms, then you have the courage to relinquish your body without suffering.

Of course, giving up one's life and body is a kind of offering that is made only in extreme situations. Only someone who has realized complete non-fear and nonattachment can take such a radical action in order to illuminate a situation of suffering. The monk Thich Quang Duc was the first person to self-immolate as an act of protest during the war, in 1963. He wanted the world to become aware of the persecution of Buddhists in Vietnam. President Dinh Diem, a Catholic, had banned the celebration of Vesak, the Buddha's birthday. Christmas was a national holiday in a country where ninety percent of the population practiced Buddhism, yet we were forbidden to celebrate Vesak. Thich Quang Duc was involved in the nonviolent struggle to restore human rights and freedom of religion. He wrote many compassionate letters, urging the government to stop the persecution of the Buddhists, but the suppression continued. One day he asked another monk to drive him to a busy intersection in the Cholon district of Saigon. He poured gasoline on himself, sat down in the street in the lotus position, and struck a match.

Within a few hours images of the monk's burning body had been published in newspapers in many countries. In this way people all over the world learned about the persecution and suffering of the Vietnamese people. A month or two later, the Diem regime was brought down by the military, and the policy of discrimination against Buddhism ended.

I knew Thich Quang Duc personally. As a young monk I practiced with him in a Sangha in central Vietnam and for a time I stayed at his temple near Saigon. In 1963, I was in New York teaching at Columbia University, and I learned of his death from an article and picture in the *New York Times*. Many people asked me, "Isn't such an act a violation of the Buddhist precept of not killing?" So I wrote Reverend Martin Luther King, Jr. a letter explaining that the monk's act was not suicide. A suicidal person is someone who is so overwhelmed by despair that they don't want to live anymore. I knew that Thich Quang Duc loved life, and wished only for his friends and all living beings to be able to live in peace.

When Jesus died on the cross he did so for the sake of human beings. His sacrifice was not made out of despair but out of the wish to help, out of his great love for humankind. That is exactly what motivated Thich Quang Duc. He acted not out of despair but from hope and love. He was free enough to offer his body in order to transmit the message to the world that the Vietnamese people were suffering, that we needed help. Because of his great compassion he was able to sit very still as the flames engulfed him, in perfect samadhi, in perfect concentration.

Such an act is a very profound offering. What is being offered? The manifestation in action of our bodhichitta, our aspiration to practice wholeheartedly and realize enlightenment in order to help bring all living beings to the shore of liberation. The sutra tells us that after Bodhisattva Seen with Joy by All Living Beings had attained samadhi, he felt overjoyed and made many kinds of offerings to the Buddha to show his great gratitude and devotion for having received the teachings. But, the sutra says, "After he had made this offering, he arose from samadhi and thought to himself, 'Though by resort to supernatural power I made an offering to the Buddha, it is not as if I had made an offering of my own body.'"[6]

The bodhisattva wanted to offer something more, the most precious thing—his own body. He had realized a level of non-fear and non-attachment, no fear and no death. This body was not his only body. When the cloud changes form it becomes rain, and when the rain transforms there is snow. The snow melts and returns to its ultimate nature as water, which becomes, once again, a cloud. Nothing at all is lost. In the sutra, it says that when the bodhisattva burnt his form body, the light from the fire of the immolation shone out through worlds as numerous as the sands of eighteen million River Ganges. The bodhisattva's body burned for "a thousand two hundred years" until it was completely consumed. This light was an awakening and an offering of the Dharma. The bodhisattva shined his light about him so that everyone could see as he could see, giving them the opportunity to see the deathless nature of the ultimate

So we have to understand this kind of offering in its proper context. In a time of great suffering, such as in Vietnam during the war, there were many such bodhisattvas among us. One of the first six members of the original Order of Interbeing in Vietnam was a young woman named Nhat Chi Mai, "one branch of plum." She was my disciple. Nhat Chi Mai immolated herself in order to call for the cessation of the hostilities between north and south. Massive destruction was taking place everywhere. Many people were dying every day from the heavy bombing. There were 500,000 American troops in Vietnam and American officials had declared that they were going to "bomb North Vietnam back to the Stone Age." Many in our group were very close to despair. The young people came to me and asked, "Thây, is there any hope that the war will end?" I didn't know what to tell them. I practiced mindfulness of breathing for a few minutes and finally I said, "The Buddha taught that everything is impermanent. The war is also impermanent, it must end one day."

This is the situation in which Nhat Chi Mai chose to make an offering of her own body. She took this action without consulting anyone. She left behind letters to her parents and her friends, as well as written appeals calling on the warring parties to stop. She knew that the police would confiscate her letters and suppress her appeals for peace and reconciliation, so she had photocopied her letters and given them to a friend to distribute after her death.

She sent me a letter, which I still have. It reads, "Dear Thây, please don't worry. Peace will surely come." That's all. She wrote this only a few hours before she burned herself. She was about to die yet she was thinking only of us, she didn't want us to worry. It is clear that her act was motivated by true love, not despair.

I was in Paris at the time. I wrote my friends in the Buddhist community and asked them to offer commemorations of Nhat Chi Mai. One friend was known as the Coconut Monk, because he liked to practice meditation on a platform up in a coconut tree; it's very fresh and cool up there. The Coconut Monk had studied in France and had become an engineer but when he returned to Vietnam he chose to become a monk. In response to my letter inviting commemorations of Nhat Chi Mai, he wrote a very moving tribute: "Mai, my niece, [he called her "niece" in the Vietnamese manner] I am burning myself like you. The only difference is that I am burning myself more slowly."

The Coconut Monk was saying, "Like yours, my life is also devoted to peace." In fact, he did many things to educate people about peace, although at the time many people thought that his actions were not very enlightened. But when we look deeply we will see that his actions were all very meaningful. He organized a practice center and invited people to come and practice sitting meditation. He collected all the bullets and the fragments of bombs in the area, melted them down, and cast a bell of mindfulness from the metal. He hung the bell in his practice center and invited it to sound every morning and evening. In a ceremony of consecration he said, "Dear bullets, dear bombs, I have helped you to come together in order to practice. In your former life you have killed but in this life you serve to call people to wake up, to wake up to humanity, to love, to understanding." This was a very beautiful and meaningful act.

The Coconut Monk went to the palace of President Thieu to bring a message of peace, but the guard would not allow him to enter. He had brought a mouse and a cat, and he sat and kept both creatures calm, so that the cat did not try to attack the mouse.

The guard said, "Go away, you cannot keep sitting here. Why are you here?" The monk said, "I want to show the president that even a cat and a mouse can live peacefully together." He was put in jail, and while there he used his own food to feed the animals. A week later he said to another prisoner, "This cat, although it doesn't get enough food every day and it could eat the mouse, has not done so. So why do we human beings fight each other and kill one another in this cruel way?" That was the action of the Coconut Monk.

A psychotherapist might think that someone who acted like this was disturbed or delusional. But that wasn't the case. In fact he was quite lucid. He took such actions in order to get a message across. In commemorating Nhat Chi Mai, he spoke of burning with the wish to help all beings—burning quickly or burning slowly—just as the body of Bodhisattva Seen with Joy by All Living Beings took thousands of years to burn, and all that time he was educating people, allowing them to look deeply into the ultimate reality of no birth, no death.

After his body had been totally consumed by the fire, the bodhisattva was reborn as a prince and at the age of twenty sought out the Buddha Pure and Bright Excellence of Sun and Moon. He knelt down before the Buddha, who had been his teacher in his former life. He said, "Wonderful, dear teacher, you are still in the world!" The gatha he spoke, recorded in the *Lotus Sutra*, is still recited by monks in Vietnam during the offering of incense:

> *O most wondrous and fine of countenance,*
> *Whose bright glow illuminates all ten quarters,*
> *Formerly I have made offerings to you,*
> *And now once again I come to behold you in person*[7]

In the past, this bodhisattva had made offerings to his teacher, the Buddha Pure and Bright Excellence of the Sun and Moon. Now he has returned in order to be near his teacher again. Because of the deep connection between teacher and disciple established in a former life, the bodhisattva was born again in the land of this Buddha in order to be able to meet his teacher of old. This is the path of devotion, gratitude, and loyalty exemplified by the practice of Medicine King Bodhisattva.

The Buddha Pure and Bright Excellence of Sun and Moon responded, "Wonderful, you have returned just in time. Tonight I will enter nirvana. I will cease manifesting as a Buddha and I now entrust the Buddhadharma to you. You will stay here to continue my mission, maintaining and offering the teachings of the wonderful Dharma to all living beings throughout the universe."

Just as the practice of Never Disparaging Bodhisattva had a specific function, to remind people of their inherent Buddha nature and potential Buddhahood, Medicine King represents another aspect of practice—the practice of devotion, dedication, and love. Without devotion and constancy you cannot go very far or deep. Without this kind of affection and dedication it is quite difficult to gain insight. This is why it is very important to establish good relationships with our Sangha brothers and sisters and our teachers. We should not underestimate the practice of devotion, but devotion alone is not enough—it must go together with the practice of meditation, of looking deeply, and the practice of compassion in action. The great bodhisattvas presented in the action dimension of the *Lotus Sutra* offer us examples of the many ways and forms of practice through which we can become the hands and arms of the Buddha in the world.

❧ TWENTY

Wonderful Sound

In chapter Twenty-Four of the *Lotus Sutra* we make the acquaintance of another bodhisattva, Wonderful Sound (Gadgadasvara). The sphere of activity of Wonderful Sound is not just the Saha world but the entire universe. Shakyamuni and Never Despising Bodhisattva are children of the Earth, and so is Avalokiteshvara, whom we will meet in the next chapter. But Bodhisattva Wonderful Sound is a guest here. He is one of the cosmic bodhisattvas visiting from other realms. From time to time, while delivering the *Lotus Sutra* on Mount Gridhrakuta, the Buddha emitted rays of light that penetrated the trichiliocosm. When Bodhisattva Wonderful Sound was touched by one of these beams of light, he saw Shakyamuni and his assembly on Vulture Peak and wanted to visit our small planet Earth to hear the teaching and pay his respects to the Buddha of the Saha world.

He asked his teacher, the Buddha Knowledge Conferred by the King of Constellations Named Pure Flower (Kamaladalvimalanakshatrarajasamkusumitabhijña), and that Buddha gave his permission for Wonderful Sound to visit Shakyamuni's world. In the cosmic realm that Wonderful Sound comes from, the bodies of the Buddhas and bodhisattvas are much larger and more glorious than those of the Earth. The sutra says that the eyes of those bodhisattvas "were like broad, great leaves of the green lotus" and that their bodies were "the color of pure gold."

So Bodhisattva Wonderful Sound's teacher told him, "My child, when you go there you must show humility. The Saha world's living beings are small and drab, and that world is not as beautiful as our cosmic realm. But don't look down on them. Buddha Shakyamuni is a great Buddha, and his assembly is also a very distinguished assembly."

Many bodhisattvas from other parts of the cosmos followed Wonderful Sound to hear the Buddha teach the *Lotus Sutra*. Before their arrival, they manifested a great number of huge, beautiful lotus blossoms all around the Gridhrakuta Mountain. The monks, nuns, laypeople, and bodhisattvas in Shakyamuni's assembly were amazed to see these beautiful lotuses suddenly appear, and they asked the Buddha to explain. He said, "There are many cosmic bodhisattvas visiting us and among them is Bodhisattva Wonderful Sound." He told them about this bodhisattva who in his former life had been a musician and composer who had served the Buddha, Dharma, and Sangha with his music.

Those of us who are musicians, composers, and singers can follow the path of Bodhisattva Wonderful Sound. Music can create harmony within us and harmony within the Sangha. Chanting, for instance, helps us concentrate and nourishes our insight, devotion, and happiness. During sitting meditation we practice a kind of music when we recite the gathas. By practicing mindful breathing, we can help the Sangha be peaceful and harmonious. This is part of our practice, making the harmonious music of mindfulness within ourselves and sharing that with others. When the Sangha comes together in silence, in deep mindful breathing, this too is a kind of silent music that we can enjoy very much. We sit together in peace and harmony, not working hard at all, just producing our being, our full presence in the Sangha, and this is enough to nourish and heal us individually and collectively. This is a kind of musical therapy that can create peace and harmony, and it has the power of healing and transformation.

Bodhisattva Wonderful Sound is someone who practices deeply this kind of music, divine music, which helps us in our practice. Like Medicine King, he has realized the samadhi of being able to appear in many emanation bodies, and he has also attained many other types of samadhi, including being able to understand the speech of all living beings. "Understanding speech" here doesn't just mean knowledge of different languages, like English, French, or Vietnamese. It means the capacity to understand at a very deep level the mental situation and inner expression of everyone, their deep longings, their suffering, their desires, and their dreams. So we can say that Bodhisattva Wonderful Sound continues the path of Bodhisattva Medicine King but he is able to go further.

Sound—music and chanting—is one of the ways of practicing the path. A painter can make an offering of color and form to the Buddha, Dharma, and Sangha. An architect can offer temples and stupas. A poet makes offerings of poems and poetic images. Bodhisattva Wonderful Sound is a musician and his music is based on awakened understanding, on his insight and samadhi. Awakened understanding is the capacity to understand the hearts of people, the inner expression as well as the words that people say. This kind of liberating music can go right to the heart of the person who hears it and transform their mind and heart. The wonderful sounds created by this bodhisattva do not conjure up grief and lament but bring about a sense of liberation, peace, and joy. Creating music that has the characteristic of awakening and liberation and that can nourish our faith is a very worthy offering to the Buddha, Dharma, and Sangha. When we sing a song of liberation, those who hear it feel their hearts lighten and give rise to joy and faith. We are following the path of Bodhisattva Wonderful Sound when we create sacred music, sacred art, or sacred language.

✆ TWENTY-ONE

Universal Gate

CHAPTER TWENTY-FIVE of the *Lotus Sutra*, "The Gateway to Everywhere of the Bodhisattva He Who Observes the Sounds of the World," is very important, it is the chapter of this sutra that is read and recited most often. It concerns the great bodhisattva of compassion, Avalokiteshvara, who is described as "the manifestation of the universal gate."

Suppose you are driving on the highway, looking for an exit that will take you into the city, or you are driving in the city and want to travel to the countryside or another city. There are many exits and roads, each leading in a different direction to a different place. On highways in France you will often see a sign that reads *toutes directions*, "all directions," and no matter where you want to go this exit will allow you to get there. That is the action of Avalokiteshvara, the universal gateway to liberation. "Universal" means the capacity to cover everything, all kinds of ground, all kinds of situations, every place and moment, all time and space. This is the kind of practice that can respond to all kinds of situations of suffering. Avalokiteshvara is the bodhisattva of love and compassion. No matter what the situation, love is the answer.

The chapter opens with a bodhisattva called Inexhaustible Mind (Akshayamati) asking the Buddha about the name of Avalokiteshvara, "For what reason is the bodhisattva...called Observer of the Sounds of the World?" The Buddha begins by describing the great powers of Avalokiteshvara, who is able to manifest in any form to help any being that calls on him. This is the subject of the prose section of the chapter. But still Akshayamati wants to know about the beautiful name of Avalokiteshvara Bodhisattva:

O World-Honored One, fully endowed with subtle signs!
  Now again I ask about that
Son of the Buddha: for what reason
  He is named the One Who Observes the Sounds of the World?

[The Buddha replied:]
Listen you to the conduct of Sound-Observer,
  The one who responds well to all places in all directions![8]

This is the definition of a universal door. The actions of Avalokiteshvara can respond to the needs of any being and any circumstance, he or she can cover all ground, all of time and space. Many people in Asia think of this bodhisattva as a female deity; in China she is known as Quan Yin. In fact, Avalokiteshvara can be male or female. As the Buddha explains in the *Lotus Sutra*, Avalokiteshvara can manifest as a businessman, as a politician, as a child, as a dragon, as a horse, as a flower—in whatever form is most appropriate to respond to the needs of the supplicant. If the situation requires the presence of Avalokiteshvara, she will be there in the most useful form in order to alleviate the suffering.

The name of this bodhisattva is sometimes rendered in Vietnamese as Quan Tu Tai. *Quan* means to observe, look deeply into, recognize. *Quan* translates the Sanskrit word *vipashyana*, and it goes with *shamatha*. Shamatha means concentrating, calming, stopping. Shamatha and vipashyana are the two elements of meditation—to stop, to concentrate, and to look deeply into the object of meditation, which may be your anger, your despair, or a difficult situation in which you find yourself. *Tu tai* means freedom. Thanks to the practice of stopping and looking deeply you attain freedom from suffering. The opening lines of the *Heart Sutra*[9] say:

> The bodhisattva Avalokiteshvara, while in the course of looking deeply, perceived that everything is empty of a separate existence. Upon that realization he became free of all affliction.

The first sentence is about looking deeply, and the second is about freedom. So the *Heart Sutra* starts out by explaining the name and practice of Avalokiteshvara—he who practices looking deeply into the ultimate nature of reality and so attains the insight that liberates him from all suffering.

Avalokiteshvara is also known as Quan The Am in Vietnamese, which means to observe, to listen, to look deeply into the sounds of the world, to hear the cries of the world, the expression of the world. Living beings express themselves in many different ways but whether or not they express themselves well, Avalokiteshvara can always understand them. Just as a child who doesn't have enough words to express himself can still be understood by his mother and father, whether someone speaks through language or bodily actions, the bodhisattva always understands.

In the *Surangama Samadhi Sutra*, it is said that Avalokiteshvara attained enlightenment through the practice of observing closely, looking deeply into the sounds of the world.[10] Usually, we speak of the object of meditation as an image that reaches us through sight, not sound. But looking deeply in this case means looking deeply into the sound that reaches our perception. The object of concentration is sound, the sound of the world, the cries of the world, because suffering often expresses itself as a cry. The *Lotus Sutra* says:

> *His broad vows as deep as the ocean*
> *Throughout kalpas beyond reckoning or discussion*
> *He has served many thousands of millions of Buddhas*
> *Uttering great and pure vows.*

Avalokiteshvara's aspiration is as wide as the ocean and was made many lifetimes in the past. He has attended many millions of Buddhas in the past and has given birth to this great, pure aspiration.

> *The hearing of his name, the sight of his body,*
> *And the recollection of him in thought do not pass away in vain,*
> *For he can extinguish the woes of existence.*

Whoever calls the name of or visualizes Avalokiteshvara in such a way that the mind becomes perfectly concentrated and pure, this person can overcome all kinds of suffering. We can begin to follow the path of this bodhisattva simply by invoking the name of Avalokiteshvara or visualizing his or her image. Calling the name of a great being is a very popular practice, not only in Buddhism but in many other spiritual traditions. In Sanskrit this practice is called *nama japa; nama* means name, and *japa* means repetition, prayer, recitation. Calling the name of the bodhisattva helps your mind become concentrated, and with concentration you become calm, lucid, mindful. The simple act of invoking the name of Avalokiteshvara in a calm and simple way can help us overcome suffering.

We can also visualize the beautiful image of that bodhisattva, riding majestically on the waves of birth and death, totally free, completely at ease, without fear. This practice is called *rupa japa*, invoking the form. Calling to mind the image of a great being also helps your mind become concentrated, mindful, and pure and helps you overcome suffering as well. What is very clear about both these practices is that you cannot do them in a machine-like way, by rote. You must call the name or visualize the form of the bodhisattva with complete presence and sincerity. Only in that way will your mind become still, calm, pure, and concentrated.

The phrase "woes of existence" in the verse means the *triloka*, the three worlds or realms of samsara.[11] Understood in terms of modern psychology, these three realms represent the different levels of the practice of mindfulness, concentration, and insight we are able to bring into our daily lives. We all experience the three realms every day. Sometimes we are in the realm of formlessness, when we feel free of attachment and clinging, no longer running after things. Sometimes we dwell in the realm of form, when we have freed ourselves of some, but not all, of our clinging and attachment. Most often we are in the realm of desire—completely caught up in attachment and clinging, always running after things, unable to experience the peace and joy of the present moment.

Whatever realm you may find yourself in, you can practice invoking the name or form of Avalokiteshvara. If you are caught in suffering, visualize the bodhisattva or call his name and let your mind become permeated by that sound or image. This practice of mindfulness will bring about concentration and then you will have a chance to get free of your suffering. This is not just *bhakti*, devotion; it is already the beginning of vipashyana, looking deeply, insight, which is founded on the practice of shamatha, stopping and concentrating the mind. You begin by calming your mind, by invoking the sound and image of Avalokiteshvara. But calling the name or visualizing the form without sincerity, humility, and faith will not create any mindfulness or tranquility.

As a young man I heard a story of a lady in North Vietnam who practiced calling the name of Amida Buddha every day, several times a day, perhaps as many as 10,000 times a day. This is the primary practice of Pure Land Buddhism, and for a sincere practitioner it can bring about much transformation and spiritual benefit. Yet this lady's practice did not change her life at all. She rang a bell, struck a drum, and burned many sticks of incense every day, but it did not bring her any deep transformation or peace. The element of diligence was there, the goodwill was there, but the practice wasn't effective because it had become rote and meaningless, a mere means to a hoped-for result rather than a deep practice of mindfulness in itself.

One day a neighbor, wanting to test her, came to the gate of her house at the time she did her practice. Just as she started to chant he began to call out to her. First she tried to ignore him but he continued to call her name, again and again. Soon she became irritated and started to strike the bell more loudly, pound harder on the drum, and chant louder. This was an indirect way of saying "Don't you know this is my practice time? Go away!" The man understood the message but continued to call her name, only now even louder. Finally she stopped chanting, put down the bell and drum, came to the door, and shouted angrily, "Why do you disturb me at a time like this? Can't you hear that I'm practicing?"

Her neighbor smiled and said, "You know, I called your name only about fifty or sixty times and you are already so upset! Every day you call the Buddha's name thousands and thousands of times, so he must be very angry at you!"

We must practice in such a way that our method of cultivating mindfulness and concentration—whether it is in the form of sitting meditation, walking meditation, chanting sutras, or invoking the name of image of a great being—serves to bring about calmness, peace, and joy. Otherwise, no matter how long or hard we practice, it will be of little or no benefit.

Now the *Lotus Sutra* describes the marvelous salvific powers of Avalokiteshvara:

> *Even if someone whose thoughts are malicious*
> *Should push one into a great pit of fire,*
> *By virtue of the constant mindfulness of Sound-Observer*
> *The pit of fire would turn into a pool.*

How can we understand this verse? Even if we are pushed into a pit of fire, when we know how to be mindful, how to practice the recollection of the powerful energy of Avalokiteshvara, the fire will be transformed into a cool lotus pond.

The word "fire" in this verse represents anger. Not only individuals are subject to the afflictions of anger and fear—they also occur on the levels of communities, societies, and nations. Sometimes an entire country can be plunged into a pit of fire. The September 11 attacks in New York and Washington, D.C. triggered a huge sea of anger, despair, and fear, and the whole United States was in danger of plunging into that pit of fire. Many Americans were looking at their televisions, listening to the inflammatory rhetoric of the politicians, and desiring revenge and retaliation. They were not able to stop and cultivate the mindfulness to look deeply into the situation in the weeks and months after the devastating event.

Yet not all Americans participated in this upwelling of anger, fear, and despair. I was in New York at the time, with friends, and we shared the insight that we cannot respond effectively to anger with anger. Violence should not be used to counter violence, that we must practice looking deeply to see the situation clearly and act with wisdom and compassion. Many people contacted me in the days immediately after the attacks; people who were practicing in order to help the nation remain calm. An angry, violent reaction could trigger a war. I began a fast, and invited friends in Europe, America, and elsewhere to join me in the fast in order to practice calming and looking deeply. I contacted congressmen, politicians, and others, including Ambassador Andrew Young (who sat with me during interviews), who shared the view that we should not attack out of anger. Over two thousand people attended the talk I gave at the Riverside Church soon after the attacks, and over a thousand were turned away for lack of space.[12]

Some politicians publicly expressed the desire to support this view, but in the political climate of retaliation, they felt unable to do so. And there were many others who shared this view but did not have enough courage to speak out. The wisdom was there, the compassion was there, but the environment was not favorable for the expression of that wisdom and compassion. Yet not all Americans shared the viewpoint of the president or supported the government's retaliatory action. We must always remember, especially in times of great turmoil or suppression, that we have more friends with us than we may think.

The message of Buddhism is very clear—*all* violence is injustice. Escalation of anger and violence leads only to more violence and anger, and in the end to total destruction. Violence and hatred can only be neutralized by compassion and loving-kindness. When you find yourself in a difficult situation, when you are about to fall into a pit of fire, if you know how to practice mindfulness of compassion and invoke the embodiment of compassion, Avalokiteshvara, then you will be able to stop, calm yourself, and look more deeply and clearly into your situation. Anger and the desire for retaliation and revenge will subside and you will be able to find the better way to respond. Understanding that we inter-are, and that any violence done to another is ultimately violence done to ourselves, we practice mindfulness of compassion so as not to cause more suffering to ourselves, our own people, or those on the so-called other side."

The ocean of fire, the pit of suffering, fear, and anger is a reality. The suffering and despair of the world is enormous, and the desire to punish those who harm us, to retaliate out of our fear and anger, is very strong in us. All of this causes the pit of fire to grow larger and it threatens to consume us all. We can turn the ocean of fire into a cool lake by practicing mindfulness of love and invoking the messenger of love, Avalokiteshvara. As the *Lotus Sutra* tells us, the bodhisattva of compassion has many aspects and can manifest in many forms and with many names. He is the universal gateway to the path of compassion and reconciliation, and through mindfulness of love, understanding, and compassion the ocean of fire is transformed into a cool, refreshing lotus pond.

Many Forms

BUDDHISM SPEAKS of the four skillful means of a bodhi-sattva. The first skillful means is making the three kinds of offerings: material gifts, the gift of the Dharma, and the gift of non-fear. When you offer good things to people they have sympathy with you, they regard you favorably, and their hearts are open. Giving someone a book on the Dharma, or a CD of some beautiful music that can help them relax—this is the practice of giving, *dana*. But the offerings of a bodhisattva should not be only material things or Dharma teachings. The best, most precious gift we can give someone is the gift of non-fear, *abhaya*.

People live in fear of death; they are afraid of losing their selfhood, their identity, of disappearing and becoming nonexistent. So when you offer the kind of teaching, practice, and insight that helps someone touch their ultimate dimension and get free of the fear of being and nonbeing, that is the greatest gift you can offer them.

The second skillful means of the bodhisattva is to practice loving speech. You can be very firm and uncompromising, but you can still use loving speech. You don't have to shout or become hostile to get your idea across. Loving speech can convey your feeling and idea to the other person in a way they are able to hear it and take it in more fully. The third skillful means is to always act to benefit others. You do whatever you can to help the other person in any situation. That is the action of the bodhisattva. The fourth skillful means is the practice of "doing the same thing." This has to do with the bodhisattva's ability to take on the appropriate form in order to be able to approach others and help them. You look like them, dress like them, do exactly what they do, you become one of them so that they will trust and accept you and have the opportunity to learn the path of understanding and love. These are the four skillful means by which the bodhisattva embraces and serves living beings.

The dimension of action of Avalokiteshvara, the universal door, is to be present everywhere at all times and manifest in innumerable forms. In many Asian Buddhist temples, there is a statue of Avalokiteshvara Bodhisattva with a thousand arms. Each arm holds an instrument or object that represents a different sphere of activity in which the bodhi-sattva can manifest compassion and understanding. In one hand he holds a book—a sutra text or a book on political science. Another hand holds a ritual instrument, such as a bell. Another holds a musical instru-ment. A modern version of the thousand-armed bodhisattva might hold a computer in one hand.

Perhaps the bodhisattva holds a gun in one of its thousand hands. Is it possible to carry a weapon and yet remain deeply a bodhisattva? This is possible. At the gates of temples in Vietnam, you often see two figures: on the left is a statue of a very gentle bodhisattva, smiling, wel-coming, while on the right is a figure with a very fierce expression, brandishing a weapon. In Vietnamese the name of this figure means lit-erally "burning-face bodhisattva"—his face is burning, his eyes are burning, fire and smoke are coming out of his eyes and mouth.[13] This is the archetype of the fierce, guardian bodhisattva, one who has the capacity to keep the hungry ghosts in check. When we offer ceremo-nial food and drink to the hungry ghosts, we evoke this bodhisattva to come and help because the hungry ghosts bring so much noise and disorder with them. We need the burning-face bodhisattva; we need his ferocity to help establish order, because only he can tame the wild hungry ghosts. He is a kind of police-chief bodhisattva.

Yet this fierce-looking character is a manifestation of Avalokitesh-vara, who takes various forms—as a gentle, motherly bodhisattva, or as a fierce guardian bodhisattva, even as a hungry ghost—in order to bet-ter understand and communicate with those he or she has come to help. Some of these manifestations may not look to us like our usual idea of a bodhisattva. If we look for Avalokiteshvara only in a nice, gentle appearance we may miss him. We have to look deeply in order to recognize the bodhisattva of compassion in his or her many forms—

as a child or adult, man or woman, as an artist, politician, musician, judge, gardener, police officer, Dharma teacher, the head of a big corporation, or a gang member.

In order to approach others to help them transform, you have to become a part of their world so that they will recognize and accept you. Then you can begin to help transform their hearts. This is the fourth skillful means of the bodhisattva, the practice of "doing the same thing." In a gang, you may look, act, and speak like any other gang member but really you are a bodhisattva. In a prison you manifest yourself as prisoner, and become a bodhisattva among prisoners. This is the action of Avalokiteshvara.

Just as "burning-face" bodhisattva carries a weapon and is a manifestation of the bodhisattva of compassion, when we see someone who carries a gun we cannot automatically say that he or she is evil. Society needs some people to serve as guardians because there are those who will behave in harmful and destructive ways toward others if there is no one to embody discipline, security, and order. So someone who carries a gun, such as a policeman or prison guard, can also be a bodhisattva. He or she may be very firm but deep within there is the heart of a bodhisattva. Our task is to help prison guards and policemen, as well as prisoners and gang members, recognize and cultivate their bodhisattva nature.

I have learned a lot from a friend, a police officer who took the mindfulness trainings some years ago, about the suffering of members of the police force in America. It is very difficult for them to do this job. The constant exposure to threat and violence and the negative way many people react to them cause the hearts of police officers to harden day by day. They feel isolated, disrespected, and uncared for by society. If police officers do not have skillful means, if they don't have enough understanding and compassion, then a lot of anger, frustration, and despair build up in them. They feel that no one understands how difficult their work is because they are seen only as oppressors. Communication between the police and the community they are supposed to serve becomes stifled. And in such an atmosphere of hostility and mistrust, some members of the police abuse their authority and become oppressors.

So you can manifest yourself as a policeman or policewoman, and play the role of bodhisattva in order to bring about better communication that will lead to more understanding and compassion. A police bodhisattva might help organize a community meeting and invite people to come and hear what the life of a police officer is like. When officers go to work in the morning, their families do not know they will return home safely. Their task is to protect others and preserve order, but they know that they might also become the victim of violence. So the job of a police officer is filled with fear and uncertainty, and when you do your job with fear and anger you cannot do it well. We should understand the immense suffering of members of the police force, prison guards, and others who serve in this capacity. Many people in these professions don't enjoy their jobs, yet they continue. Avalokiteshvara must appear in their midst and try to open their hearts.

A police bodhisattva can work to reestablish communication between the police and the community, so that they can talk to and listen to one another with understanding and compassion. Communication is possible. Police officers can help non-police officers, and non-police officers can help police officers. There can be collaboration between them. There is a way through any situation, no matter how difficult. And the way that is prescribed by the teaching is to practice deep listening, to listen with compassion, and to use loving speech, one of the skillful means of the bodhisattva. Once communication is restored we have hope, and suffering will be lessened.

Avalokiteshvara shows us that even if you must be very firm, even when you have to carry a weapon or impose authority, at the same time you can be very compassionate. You can serve as a fierce burning-face bodhisattva with a tender heart and deep understanding. This is how you can be a bodhisattva in that form. But to serve as any kind of bodhisattva—a tender, motherly bodhisattva or a fierce guardian bodhisattva—you have to really *be* a bodhisattva. You can't just act the part, merely appearing to be a bodhisattva outwardly while inwardly your heart is closed. You must have real understanding and compassion in order to be worthy of being called a bodhisattva.

If you look closely at the figure of the thousand-armed bodhisattva you will see that in the palm of each hand there is an eye. The eye symbolizes the presence of understanding, wisdom, prajña. We need both compassion and wisdom to progress on the path. Understanding and wisdom help to bring about love, kindness, and compassion. Avalokiteshvara has so many arms because love needs to express itself in many different forms and through the use of many kinds of instruments. That is why every arm is holding a different instrument and in every hand there is the eye of wisdom.

Sometimes we may believe that we are acting from love but if our action is not based in deep understanding, it will bring suffering. You want to make someone happy, and you believe very strongly that you are doing something out of love. But your action may make the other person suffer very much. So even though you believe you are acting from love, you cause your son or daughter, your partner or spouse, your friend or coworker to suffer deeply because you do not have enough understanding of that person. That is why you need the eye of understanding, of wisdom, to be an effective instrument of compassion.

If you don't understand the suffering, the difficulty, the deep aspiration of another person, it's not possible for you to love them. So it's very important to check with them and ask for help. A father should be able to ask his child, "Do I understand you well enough? Do I make you suffer because of my lack of understanding?" A mother should be able to ask her child, "Do you think I understand you? Please tell me so that I can love you properly." That is the language of love. And if you are sincere, your daughter or son will tell you about their suffering. And when you have understood their suffering you will stop doing things that make him or her suffer, things that you believed you did only for her happiness and well-being. Deep understanding is the substance of which true love is made. The hands of the bodhisattva symbolize action, but our actions must be guided well by the eyes of understanding.

Some of us serve as bodhisattvas with several arms. We take care of our family, and at the same time we are able to participate in the work of protecting the environment and helping others in the world. All of us are capable of being present in many places in the world. You can be here and at the same time, through your compassionate action, you can be in a prison, or in a remote country where the children suffer from malnutrition. You don't have to be present in those other places with your physical body because you have many transformation bodies that can serve everywhere.

When I write a book I transform myself into a multitude of forms—the ideas and words in the book—in order to go everywhere. Every book I offer is one of my transformation bodies. I can go into a cloister in the form of a book or inside a prison in the form of an audiotape. Each of us has many transformation bodies, and that is why it is so important to learn to recognize our transformation bodies. Being a bodhisattva is not abstract but a very concrete practice that we can do—just like Avalokiteshvara, we manifest ourselves in many bodies, many forms, in order to help as many people as possible.

You have to be very awake to recognize the bodhisattva in his various forms. Avalokiteshvara may be very close to you right now. You may be able to touch him just by reaching out your hand. Compassion does exist, understanding does exist. It is possible for us to cultivate the energy of compassion and understanding so that Avalokiteshvara can be with us at all times, in our daily life, and we will be well protected with understanding and compassion.

TWENTY-THREE

Mindfulness of Love

THE VERSES in Chapter Twenty-Five of the *Lotus Sutra* go on to describe how the Universal Gate is able to deliver us from a variety of dangerous situations. In every case, the key to our salvation is mindfulness—mindfulness of love and of the embodiment of love and compassion, bodhisattva Avalokiteshvara. "By virtue of constant mindfulness of Sound-Observer," the sutra tells us, we will be delivered from all danger and suffering.[14] Mindfulness is the key that allows us to discern and act wisely, to respond appropriately, to know what and what not to do in a dangerous situation in order to bring about the best result.

Looking deeply and practicing the mindfulness of love helps us to be lucid, to be loving, and that lucidity and loving kindness serve as a kind of protection for us, keeping us from all kinds of danger. We usually believe that danger comes to us from outside. Yet most of the danger we face comes from within ourselves. Without a clear view, our fear and misunderstanding can create a lot of dangerous situations. Delusion, anger, and craving—the "three poisons"—are the basic afflictions and they can be healed and transformed by the practice of mindfulness of love. Mindfulness of love can help stop suffering right away and lead us away from the poisonous fires.

We know that compassion must be informed by understanding, and wisdom *prajña*, because without understanding, deep compassion is impossible. That is why the practice of compassion begins with the practice of looking deeply, *vipashyan*a. When we practice mindfulness, we gain a deeper understanding of the situation and from that deeper understanding compassion naturally flows. Prajña will bring *maitri*—love, kindness, and compassion.

If you are in a conflict with another person, the first thing you should do is to seek to understand him deeply. Looking deeply, you will see into his suffering and you will not want to harm him, punish him, or make him suffer anymore. You will accept him as he is and try to help him. This is how understanding helps love to be possible. And love also helps our understanding to deepen. When you feel sympathy and love for someone, you are in a better position to understand him or her. If you don't have any empathy for that person, if you don't accept her, then you will have no chance for understanding. Affection and love help us along the path of prajña and increase our energy of understanding. Understanding and love are interdependent. Love is made of understanding and understanding is made of love.

Mindfulness of love can help us in so many ways. Suppose that you are driving in your car and you are aware that your child is waiting for you at home. If you practice mindfulness of love, if you think of your child waiting for you to arrive home safely, you will be more mindful and will drive more carefully and safely. Perhaps you are thinking of having a drink. Practicing mindfulness of love, you think of your child, and you know that you are going to have to drive in a few minutes. Even if you want a drink very much because it makes you feel good, practicing mindfulness of love will help you choose not to drink at that moment. It's a good practice to put a picture of your child or anyone you love on the dashboard of your car so that when you drive you will be reminded to practice mindfulness of love and you will drive carefully.

You can keep a picture of the one you love with you in your wallet, or in a place where you can see it often. That picture may be of the Buddha or a bodhisattva, your daughter or son, your spouse or partner, even a beloved pet. Any being that you love can inspire you to be more mindful, to take care of yourself. And by taking good care of yourself you take good care of your beloved. This is a practice of mindfulness of love. You don't have to be a very religious person or do a lot of devotional practices. You just have to call to mind those you love.

Calling the name of Avalokiteshvara is one of the ways to awaken the energy of compassion in our heart. When something or someone offers you freshness, joy, and loving-kindness, the image of that person or thing can become the object of your mindfulness. Not only a person but also a place can embody compassion and understanding. Suppose you go to Plum Village and enjoy the setting, the environment, and the Sangha life there. Even when you are away from Plum Village, every time you remember it you recall to yourself some of the freshness and joy of the place. So recalling the form, sight, or sound of a manifestation of compassion helps you suffer less. Every time you think of her, every time you are mindful of him, every time you see in your mind's eye that beautiful place, then immediately the element of compassion and understanding is born in your heart. Mindfulness of love is the practice that can call up the nectar of compassion and understanding in us, and help us avoid all kinds of dangers.

When you are caught in desire, mindfulness of compassion can help free you from the entanglement. In Chinese translations of the sutras, "desire" is clearly rendered as sexual desire. But the term actually applies to all kinds of craving—craving for fame, power, wealth, and so on. When you run after money, fame, and power, when you allow the flame of craving to burn in you, you suffer a lot. And if you don't know how to practice, the fire of inappropriate sexual desire can also burn you and make you suffer. How can mindfulness of love and compassion help you to suffer less?

Before you begin a sexual relationship with someone, practice mindfulness. Look deeply into the situation of the other person and yourself. Will the act destroy your lives, or create a lot of suffering for the people you love, for your family? Awareness and mindfulness bring understanding and wisdom. And wisdom brings about love and wise conduct, the understanding that helps you refrain from making actions that will lead to suffering. This is how mindfulness of compassion can keep you from getting burned by the flame of desire.

A good teacher knows that if he or she transgresses and violates the third mindfulness training by having an affair with one of his or her students, it will destroy that person, destroy the Sangha, and destroy their ideal of compassion. As a teacher, you know that the happiness and well-being of the Sangha depends on your behavior and you don't want the community to suffer. This is very natural. So it's very easy to practice the third mindfulness training when we think of it as a practice of love. Perfecting the practice of the precepts (shila), one of the six paramitas of the bodhisattva, is not accomplished through hard work or struggle but through the energy of compassion in you. Awareness, mindfulness, and compassion make the practice of the mindfulness trainings very easy. Once love is in your heart you don't have to do anything, you can practice the mindfulness trainings perfectly, very easily, without any struggle at all.

Every time the energy of mindfulness of compassion is born in your heart you can be free from craving. It's like a miracle, not hard labor. The practice of love, mindfulness of love, is quite wonderful. It really is a universal gate. Compassion makes it possible for us to relate to other people and other living beings in the best possible ways. That is why the practice aims at making the nectar of compassion flow. Without compassion we will become completely dried up, utterly alone and isolated. People who do not have compassion suffer most in the world. They are terribly lonely. Those who behave cruelly, who do not have love and compassion in themselves, suffer quite a lot. They need our help, not punishment or retaliation.

Many Vietnamese people have experienced the particular suffering of war, and we know that war involves a lot of cruelty. During the war in Vietnam, American operatives tortured Vietnamese guerilla fighters in order to get information. The CIA's function is to gather information; it is the central "intelligence" agency. But are such methods really intelligent? Intelligence has to do with wisdom, with understanding. Without understanding, you will not be able to have compassion. If you are really intelligent you know that creating suffering for others will only bring more danger and suffering back to yourself. Any violence we do to another person is in fact an act of violence against ourselves. If you don't understand this basic truth, you will suffer more and more.

When you have been a victim of torture it's very difficult not to have anger toward those who harmed you. And American veterans suffer deeply because of the fact that they have killed and maimed people. How can we help both the victims and perpetrators of violence? Through mindfulness of compassion, mindfulness of love. We can look with the eyes of love at the person who is causing us to suffer: "This person in front of me, even though he has done cruel things against me and others, even though he has lost touch with his humanity, is himself a victim of violence and cruelty. I will practice to be able to see him with the eyes of love and help him get in touch with his humanity."

Without compassion and love you'll be overwhelmed by anger and hatred toward the person who has harmed you. There are those who are so cruel, who have done such terrible things, that you cannot believe they are human beings. There are many people like this in the world, in South America, in North America, in Africa, in Europe, in the Middle East, in Asia, everywhere. You may think that if you had a gun in your hand you would shoot someone like that right then and there. But would you shoot a Buddha? We know from the *Lotus Sutra* that *everyone* has the seed of Buddhahood. And we know that meeting hatred with hatred, meeting violence with vengeance and retaliation can never lead to the end of hatred and violence. Love is the only force that can protect ourselves and others from harm.

The first thing you notice when practicing mindfulness of compassion is that you don't suffer anymore. When you have enough of the energy of compassion and love in you, your heart grows big and you can embrace everything and everyone—even those you call your enemy. When you can look deeply into your "enemy" and see that he is a victim of ideas, notions, and misinformation, of conditions in his own life and his culture and society, then you can remain calm, your heart remains open, and you will have a better chance to help him get in touch with his humanity, his innate Buddha nature, and transform the seeds of hatred and violence within.

The practice of Avalokiteshvara allows us to listen and look deeply in order to understand. With understanding, compassion arises in our hearts and we know what to do in order to help.

Non-Fear

P ERHAPS AS A CHILD you played with a very simple, wonder-ful toy called a kaleidoscope. It makes a very beautiful pattern of colors and shapes, and when you turn it a little bit the pattern is replaced by another set of colors and shapes. Every manifestation is wonderful and beautiful, and they are always changing. A child does-n't feel regret when one manifestation gives way to another, she just enjoys each manifestation as it is, because each one emerges from the same ground, the bits of color in the kaleidoscope.

The ground of all manifestation, the ultimate dimension, is always there. The role of the bodhisattva in the action dimension is to help us get in touch with our ultimate dimension, offer us the gift of non-fear. The different colors and shapes, the variety of forms and manifestations, are only various kinds of appearances. When you can touch the ultimate dimension of yourself and everything, you no longer feel fear. You are not caught by attachment to a particular manifestation, by notions of birth and death, being or nonbeing, because you know that this body, this form is just one manifestation. You are ready to manifest again in another form, quite as wonderful as this one.

To be a cloud floating in the sky is wonderful. But to be rain falling on the earth and into the rivers is also wonderful. To be snow on a mountaintop is also wonderful. To be water for a child to drink is also wonderful. Water can manifest itself in many different forms and every form is wonderful, every manifestation is necessary. Bodhisattvas are not caught in one manifestation, in one body, so they can give up their body very easily, just as Medicine King Bodhisattva gave up his body and allowed it to burn for thousands of years in order to offer the teaching to many beings.

Each manifestation is linked to the next manifestation in terms of cause and effect. If the cloud is polluted, the rain will also be polluted. That is why the practice of self-purification is so important. While being a cloud you try your best to practice self-purification so that your next manifestation will be beautiful. When you fall to the earth as rain you will be very pure, delicious water. By transforming ourselves through self-purification we help to purify the world.

We know we draw danger to ourselves because of the deluded way we perceive reality. We have blocks of craving, anger, and delusion in ourselves that make it impossible to see the ultimate dimension. That is why self-purification, learning to look deeply in order to remove our anger, craving, and delusion, is necessary in order to allow us to get in touch with the ultimate dimension. When we are able to touch the ultimate dimension we are no longer afraid of anything, we can offer our understanding and compassion to transform any situation of danger and suffering.

I know a nun and a monk in Vietnam, former students of mine, who were arrested because of their work on behalf of human rights. The monk was charged with treason and sentenced to death. Thanks to international pressure the government lifted the death sentence, but he remains under house arrest. This gentle monk has the energy of non-fear in him. He's ready to give up his body for his belief in the basic human rights of the Vietnamese people. He has the wisdom of the ultimate dimension.

The nun also spent a long time in prison, and she continued her practice of walking and sitting meditation in her small cell. Thanks to the practice she remained relaxed, calm, and cheerful. Anger and despair were not able to take root in her, and she was able to help the other prisoners, many of whom were very hostile toward the prison guards. The guards treated her kindly—not because she is a nun but because she embodies mindfulness of compassion. She did not let herself become a victim of anger and craving and so she was able to make very good use of her time in prison. It became a kind of retreat—she didn't have to do anything, just enjoy the practice. Instead of experiencing prison as a pit of fire, she transformed it into a cool lotus pond through the practice of mindfulness, compassion, and understanding.

If we find ourselves in a situation like this, and if we know how to practice the universal gate, mindfulness of compassion, we won't suffer and we can even help others who are in the same situation—not just fellow prisoners but those on the "other side," the prison administrators, the guards, and so on.

The verses in chapter Twenty-Five of the *Lotus Sutra* describe how Avalokiteshvara's understanding and compassion bring about transformation and healing:

> *The beings suffer embarrassment and discomfort;*
>   *Incalculable woes press in upon them.*
> *The Sound-Observer, by virtue of his unblemished knowledge,*
>   *Can rescue the world from its woes.*[15]

There is so much suffering in the world. Through the understanding and knowledge gained by closely observing the sounds of the world, Avalokiteshvara helps not just in one way but in many ways to alleviate suffering and bring living beings to the shore of liberation.

> *He is fully endowed with the power of supernatural penetration*
>   *And broadly cultivates wisdom and expedient devices.*
> *In the lands of all ten quarters*
>   *There is no kshetra where he does not display his body.*[16]

Avalokiteshvara's wisdom and his capacity to use skillful means are immense. Through his great wisdom, he invents various skillful means in order to help in as many ways and as many forms as needed. He manifests himself in innumerable emanation bodies in many places, many lands, everywhere. We too can also be present in many places at one time, through our transformation bodies. You can be practicing in a Sangha and at the same time be somewhere else, performing some action, in the form of a friend or a student, or in something you have written, created, or offered. Your hands can reach very far.

> *O you of the true gaze, of the pure gaze,*
>   *Of the gaze of broad and great wisdom,*
> *Of the compassionate gaze and the gaze of goodwill!*

This verse describes the five kinds of gazes of Avalokiteshvara. First is the contemplation of the true nature of things, *satya*. When you are calm, when you are lucid, you have the capacity to recognize the ultimate dimension. It's followed by the contemplation on purification, *visuddhi vimala*. We need the practice of self-purification, just as the cloud in the sky has to become pure rain for the sake of the world. Third is the contemplation on great wisdom, *mahaprajña*. This is not mere knowledge but the realization of true wisdom, *mahaprajña-paramita*—the great wisdom that has the power to bring you to the other shore, the shore of safety, the shore of non-fear, the shore of liberation. Fourth is the contemplation on compassion, *karuna*. Fifth is the contemplation on loving-kindness—*maitri*. Like Avalokiteshvara, we should practice mindfulness of and reverence for these five qualities.

> *The thunder of the monastic prohibitions, whose essence is goodwill,*
> *And the great subtle cloud, which is the sense of compassion,*
> *Pour forth the Dharma-rain of sweet dew,*
> *Extinguishing and removing the flames of agony.*

This is a very beautiful verse. The practice of the mindfulness trainings, which help establish in us the elements of loving-kindness, maitri, goodwill, is like thunder. The element of compassion is like a wonderful great thundercloud. These qualities are not something soft but very strong and powerful. The two images, "thunder" and "cloud," come together and produce rain, the Dharma rain. The compassionate rain of the Dharma falls down like nectar, extinguishing all the fires of affliction.

> *The delicate-voiced One Who Observes the Sounds of the World*
> *And the Brahma-voiced sound of the tide*
> *Are superior to the sounds of the world*
> *Therefore one must be ever mindful of them.*

This verse speaks about the different kinds of sound of the bodhisattva. There is the "delicate-voiced" sound of the One Who Observes the Sounds of the World, the bodhisattva who practices looking deeply into the world. All of us who are friends of the Buddha, practice just the same. We try to look deeply into the world to understand better. That is the meaning of meditation—to look deeply into what is there. And looking deeply in this way, observing the sounds of the world, we come to understand it and to understand ourselves, and we become free from afflictions of craving, delusion, and anger.

Then there is the sound of nobility, *brahma*. Avalokiteshvara emits a wonderful sound, clear and noble. Some sounds are low and heavy, containing craving or despair. But as a practitioner on the path of self-purification, the sound you emit every day becomes finer, more clear and pure. Every cell of your body, every mental formation in you is on the way to purification and transformation.

Next is the sound of the tide. The teaching of the Buddha is likened to the powerful sound of the rising tide. The sound of the tide is very powerful. The sound of the rising tide can embrace and take away all the other sounds that are low and heavy, leaving only the clear, high, noble sound of the teachings.

The sound emitted by the bodhisattva that can transcend all the other sounds of the world is the sound that reveals to us the dharmadhatu, the realm of ultimate reality. It transcends and surpasses all the sounds that belong to the *lokadhatu*, the realm of the world of perception and form, the historical dimension. When we can tune into these various kinds of sounds, they have the capacity for transformation and healing.

These verses show us how to practice mindfulness of Avalokiteshvara to get in touch with these five kinds of contemplation and different kinds of sound that are the essence of the bodhisattva. Avalokiteshvara is not a god, but just a name for a real person with a real practice and real qualities. These verses are an encouragement for us to diligently practice mindfulness of Avalokiteshvara in order to get in touch with these virtues and cultivate them in ourselves.

> *From moment to moment conceive no doubts,*
> *For the pure saint Who Observes the Sounds of the World*
> *In the discomforts of pain, agony, and death*
> *Can be a point of reliance.*

Dwell in mindfulness every moment, without any doubt about the power of compassion and understanding. With great confidence and faith in Avalokiteshvara, every moment is a moment of mindfulness with compassion and understanding as its object. The symbol of compassion becomes the object of your mindfulness, the object of your recollection. And even in a situation of danger, "of pain, agony, and death," you maintain this awareness and recollection.

Avalokiteshvara is a holy person, but holiness is not something we find only in certain persons. Everywhere that there is mindfulness, concentration, and insight there is the element of holiness. So when we take the qualities of Avalokiteshvara as the object of our mindfulness, then the element of holiness arises in us too. With Avalokiteshvara as our refuge and protection, we reach the shore of non-fear, no longer afraid of danger or suffering, no longer in fear of death.

> *Fully endowed with all the merits,*
>   *His benevolent eye beholding the beings,*
> *He is happiness accumulated, a sea incalculable.*
>   *For this reason one must bow one's head to him.*

This is the concluding verse of the chapter. The bodhisattva of compassion is equipped with all kinds of merits (*sattva punya*), acquired during countless lifetimes of manifesting understanding and compassion. He is able to regard all beings with love and compassion. I think this is the most beautiful sentence in the entire sutra: The bodhisattva regards all beings with the eyes of love. You too have the eyes of compassion and love. The Buddha eye has been transmitted to you. The question is whether you will choose to make use of those eyes to look deeply.

Looking deeply, listening carefully, you understand the suffering of the other person, you accept him or her, and naturally your love and compassion flow freely. This is the most beautiful practice, the most powerful method of bringing about transformation and healing. Happiness is not described here in terms of weights or measures, but as a vast, incalculable ocean.

Happiness is made of one substance—compassion. If you don't have compassion in your heart you cannot be happy. Cultivating compassion for others, you create happiness for yourself and for the world. And because Avalokiteshvara is the embodiment of this practice and the sutra says that we pay respect to him by bowing and touching our foreheads to the ground. This is an ancient Indian practice, a gesture of deep respect to one's teacher.

Love can manifest itself in many forms, and we have to apply our understanding and intelligence in order to recognize compassion and love in its many different guises. In the *Avatamsaka Sutra* there is the notion of a kind of door with two aspects: the main figure and the secondary figure. During the teaching of the *Lotus Sutra* on the Gridhrakuta Mountain, Shakyamuni played the main role, that of the Buddha, and Avalokiteshvara played the secondary role of a bodhisattva disciple.

We know that Avalokiteshvara is already a Buddha, a fully enlightened being. But if there is a teacher there must be students, and if there are students there must be a teacher. So the Buddhas and bodhisattvas take turns at appearing as teacher or student. Sometime later you'll be a teacher and I will be your student. This is the way that a living Sangha functions. Think of a formation of white geese in the sky. If the lead bird becomes tired, he slows down and lets another bird advance to be leader. Sometimes you play the main role, the role of the leader; sometimes you play the role of a follower. Yet there is no discrimination at all, you are equally happy in each role. You are happy being a teacher, and happy to be a student. In the *Lotus Sutra*, Avalokiteshvara has played the role of student very well. But if we look deeply into the personality, actions, and wisdom of this bodhisattva, we know that no one can surpass him in terms of compassion and understanding.

ॐ TWENTY-FIVE

Earth-Holder and Earth-Store

At THE END of chapter Twenty-Five of the *Lotus Sutra*, a
lay bodhisattva named Dharanimdhara is mentioned.
His name means "to hold, to protect, to preserve the Earth." In English, we could call this bodhisattva Protector of the Earth, or Earth-
Holder. This bodhisattva helps further communication between
humans and other species. He is a kind of engineer whose task is to create healthy space for us to live in, build bridges for us to connect with
one another, and build roads so that we can go to the people we love.
It is said that when the Buddha wished to visit his mother Mahamaya
in the Tushita Heaven, it was Earth-Holder who built the road that the
Buddha traveled on. Though he is only briefly mentioned in the *Lotus
Sutra*, we create a new chapter for this bodhisattva because he is greatly
needed in these times.

Earth-Holder works to preserve this planet for living beings by taking care of the air, water, and soil. Those who work to protect the environment and maintain a healthy ecosystem on this planet Earth are all
allies of this bodhisattva. We all have to become the arms and hands of
this bodhisattva in order to protect and preserve the Earth for future
generations.

The situation of our planet Earth is very alarming. The destruction
of the forests, land, water, and atmosphere continues at a very dangerous rate. The governments of most nations, focused solely on economic development, are allowing the natural environment under their
control to be exploited, polluted, and destroyed in the name of
"progress." Many species on Earth have already been destroyed, and
more are dying off every day. The rainforests, the lungs of our planet,
are being decimated. The protective layer of ozone in our atmosphere

147

is being degraded. The United Nations warns that the state of the Earth's environment is extremely precarious.

We have to take up the practice of Earth-Holder Bodhisattva and make protecting and preserving the Earth a top priority. The president, prime minister, or head of state of every nation must be made aware of the dire situation of the planet. We must work to increase awareness of the situation because only mindfulness, awareness of what is happening, can save us from the path of certain disaster we are currently on.

We cannot say that we are too busy to take up this work. Our political leaders are always too busy and seem to always focus their attention on other things, such as economic development or consolidating political power. Governments will not be able to solve the problem of the environment as long as they are concerned only with their own localized, national interests. We must help our societies and leaders see that the situation of the Earth affects all nations and peoples, and that we must all be involved in efforts to protect the environment.

In the Sixties and Seventies, our Buddhist community and friends in the peace and environmental movements worked to help increase awareness of the situation of the Earth. In 1969, sponsored by the International Fellowship of Reconciliation, a pacifist organization, we set up an organization called Dai Dong, Great Togetherness. We spoke about environmental deterioration, the depletion of natural resources, overpopulation, and hunger; we spoke about war and we spoke about what can be done to create a way out of these pressing problems. We were not acting as governments, which hold their own national interests paramount, but on behalf of all people of the Earth, in the spirit of great togetherness. At that time, there was not yet much public discussion or awareness of environmental issues. We continued holding retreats, Dharma discussions, and conferences in order to bring greater awareness. With the collaboration of scientists and environmentalists from all over the world, little by little all of us working in this way were able to bring about more awareness of the situation of the planet.

Now environmental concerns and issues are much more widely discussed and there is much greater awareness generally, yet the destruction of the Earth's land, air, and water continues. That is why

Earth-Holder Bodhisattva is very much needed in our time. Every one of us must become aware of the presence of this bodhisattva in ourselves, so that we can become the arms and hands of the bodhisattva and act quickly to protect the Earth.

If there is awareness of what is really going on, then there is the possibility that immediate steps will be taken to change the situation for the well-being of the planet. Heads of state must become more aware, must be directly exposed to the truth about the situation of our planet. All the conflicting parties in the world must be made to see that their conflicts should be resolved as quickly as possible so that all nations can collectively take the necessary action to save the planet.

In my mind I have the image of a number of chickens in a small cage, fighting over the bits of food inside, unaware that in a few hours they will all be killed. So many of us concern ourselves only about the prosperity and economic development of our own community or nation that we don't realize the gravity of the global situation. If we become aware of what is happening to the planet Earth, then we would stop our international disputes and turn to the greater work of healing the planet that is home to us all.

There is another bodhisattva mentioned in the *Lotus Sutra*, Earth-Store (Kshitigarbha). Kshitigarbha means "womb or storehouse of the Earth." The Earth is very solid and contains and preserves many kinds of jewels. So this name describes the qualities of this bodhisattva: solid, long-lasting, and preserving many virtues. Earth-Store Bodhisattva represents a realm of action that is very much needed now. Earth-Store has vowed that as long as the hells are not vacant he will not rest. He will not enter nirvana and enjoy being a Buddha. He will not stop working to lead all beings toward Buddhahood. Bodhisattva Earth-Store is someone who vows to go to the darkest places of the universe in order to rescue those who are in the most desperate straits, the situations of greatest suffering. He has vowed to go to those places where there is no freedom, no democracy, no compassion or human dignity, where there is oppression, injustice, social inequality, and war. Hell is the place where Earth-Store wants to go, because that is where the need for his help is greatest.

Many people choose to go to places of great suffering around the world to help those who are oppressed and do not have the means to live a decent life. Many young people want to leave the culture of materialism they have grown up in and do volunteer work in such places, where they can express their love, compassion, and understanding by helping to build schools, dig wells, teach, offer medical care, and so on. This is very good but in order to help in this way we don't have to go somewhere else, to a far-off foreign country. Hell is right here in our own society, and if we want to become the arms and hands of Earth-Store Bodhisattva, we have to be able to recognize the suffering of the hell realms that is everywhere within us and around us.

We can identify very easily those who are in hell and who need our help, who need the action of Earth-Store Bodhisattva. There are many hungry ghosts wandering around us all the time. Whenever we organize a ceremony to offer food and drink to the hungry ghosts, we evoke the name of this bodhisattva. We ask him to bring the hungry ghosts to us and we offer them food, drink, and the opportunity to hear the Dharma so they can transform their suffering and be born in the Pure Land of the Buddha. And we always remind Earth-Store of his great vow.

A person who is not well-rooted in his family, in his society, in his tradition, becomes a hungry ghost. He doesn't know where to go. She doesn't believe in anything or anyone. When you encounter someone like this you can recognize him or her right away, in the way they walk, the way they look, the way they behave. There's a lot of suffering in them because their roots have been cut off. They are not rooted in their family, so in effect they have no family. Perhaps when they saw how their parents acted toward each other they were not inspired to make a marriage or partnership and raise a family themselves. They don't believe in the existence of healthy, loving relationships, so they reject their families and do not form close bonds, and in doing so they suffer very much.

Other hungry ghosts are not rooted in their community or society, or in their cultural or spiritual tradition. They have left their church or synagogue or temple; they don't accept any teaching and reject faith and religion. They feel that these things are not relevant to them because they have nothing to do with the actual experience of their day-to-day lives. So they become completely alienated, cut off from anything that could offer them support and stability.

Thousands of hungry ghosts are created every day in our society. Our consumer culture emphasizes individualism and materialism over service and community, and our religious and social institutions have often lost touch with the real suffering of people and do little to help alleviate it. In some cases, these institutions become so corrupt that they end up creating even more suffering in society. As a result, there are more and more hungry ghosts everywhere around us.

In order to help a hungry ghost you have to be very patient because the habit energy of fear and mistrust is very strong in their mind and heart. When we offer them something that can satisfy their need, they don't believe it and often have a difficult time accepting our help. They are desperately hungry for understanding and love, yet they don't believe that anyone can really understand or love them. Even though they may speak about love, they don't really understand or know love and they are very suspicious. The only way help a hungry ghost is to spend a lot of time with him or her. Through your way of speaking, acting, and being with a hungry ghost over a long period of time you can gradually win their trust and then they will begin to listen to you, receive your help and understanding, and begin to transform.

It takes a long time for a hungry ghost to become rooted in a family or community. To create a hungry ghost is all too easy and happens very quickly but to heal one, to help him or her become rooted in the human community, is difficult and takes a very long time. Some suffer so much they can no longer bear it, so they try to forget their suffering in drugs, alcohol, sex, and so on, and this makes them suffer even more. We may feel we don't have the means to help such a person. Hell is there, the hungry ghost is there, but we may have no means to help, and if we don't take good care of ourselves we are in danger of becoming a hungry ghost, too. So we need to invoke the energy of Bodhisattva Kshitigarbha in order to help.

You need a lot of patience and courage to be a friend of this bodhisattva, to become his arms and hands and do his work in the world. As a follower of Earth-Store, you will meet many people like Angulimala, a murderer in the time of the Buddha. His name means "garland of fingers," because he wore a necklace strung with the fingers of his victims. So you can see that there was a lot of anger and hatred in Angulimala. He was a hungry ghost; he believed that no one loved him, that human beings were by nature cruel, dishonest, and unfaithful, and he became a thief and a murderer.

One day the Buddha went on the almsround in the city of Shravasti, and found all the houses locked. Everyone was afraid because Angulimala was in the area. One person asked the Buddha to come into his house to receive food there and not wander around outside because it was too dangerous. But the Buddha said, "It is my practice to do walking meditation and visit many homes and meet with people. I cannot just stay in one house," and he continued on his almsround.

As he was walking through the forest on his way back to the monastery, the Buddha suddenly heard the sound of someone running behind him, and a voice called out, "Monk, hey monk, stop!" The Buddha knew that it was Angulimala, but he simply continued to practice walking meditation with peace and solidity. He didn't feel afraid because he had a lot of calmness and compassion within himself. Soon Angulimala caught up with him and, falling into step next to him, said, "Monk, I told you to stop. Why didn't you stop?" The Buddha continued walking mindfully and said quietly, "Angulimala, I have already stopped a long time ago. It is you who have not stopped."

Andgulimala was quite surprised by this. No one had ever spoken to him in this way; everyone had always trembled in fear of him. He ran in front of the Buddha to force him to stop walking and said, "What do you mean by that? I told you to stop but you are still walking. You haven't stopped but you say that you have already stopped. Explain this to me."

The Buddha looked at Angulimala and said very calmly, "Angulimala, I stopped doing cruel and harmful things a long time ago. I don't want to create suffering and despair, and that is why I have learned the path of compassion and understanding. No living being wants to suffer, no living being wants to die, everyone wants to live and be happy. We should be aware of that. We should try to be compassionate and respect life and be kind to other beings. We should love others instead of hating them and killing them."

Angulimala shouted, "Human beings are very cruel. No one loves me, no one understands me. Why should I be compassionate toward them?"

The Buddha replied, "Angulimala, I agree with you that there are very cruel human beings and they have made you suffer. But I don't agree with you that all human beings are like that. There are many people who are very compassionate and kind. Have you ever met one of my monks or nuns? There are many of them in the town. They practice loving-kindness and compassion, they don't want to harm even a tiny insect. You know, when we have compassion within us we suffer much less."

Angulimala was very surprised and curious. He thought, This monk knows that I am Angulimala, yet he's not afraid of me. Maybe he is the one called Gautama I have heard of. So he asked the Buddha, "Are you Gautama, the Buddha?"

"Yes."

"Buddha, it's too late to do what you suggest."

"It's never too late to do a good thing," said the Buddha.

"What good thing can I do?" asked Angulimala.

The Buddha said, "To stop wrongdoing, stop creating suffering for yourself and others is the greatest good that you can do."

"It's too late for me. I have committed so many crimes. Even if I wanted to stop now, people wouldn't leave me in peace."

"Angulimala, if you really want to turn away from violence and follow the path of compassion and kindness, I promise to help you."

Angulimala was so moved by the Buddha's kindness and non-fear, at that very moment he threw down his sword, knelt down, and asked to become his disciple. Right then Shariputra and some of the other monks arrived. They had been out looking for the Buddha because they knew that Angulimala was around. Now they found the Buddha safe with the notorious criminal, who already had taken refuge. They were all very glad. The Buddha instructed Shariputra to cut Angulimala's hair right then and there, give him a robe to wear, and take him back to the monastery to begin training in the practice. He told Shariputra to keep him in the monastery for several weeks so he wouldn't have to go into the city on the almsround every day like the other monks. Angulimala devoted all his time to learning the practice of mindfulness, and in no time at all he became a very good monk. His transformation took place very quickly because he wanted with all his being to completely change his life.

After a month or so, the Buddha allowed Angulimala to accompany him on almsround in the city. On the way, the Buddha saw King Prasenajit speaking to a group of soldiers. The Buddha greeted the king and asked, "Majesty, are you preparing the army for a war? Is there some trouble at the frontier?

King Prasenajit said, "No, Lord, there is no war at the frontier."

"Why are you gathering an army?" asked the Buddha.

"Because I have heard that Angulimala is in town. He's a very dangerous person. One time I sent fifty soldiers into a forest after him, and he killed most of them. So I am personally directing a military operation to capture this dangerous killer."

While the Buddha was talking to the king, Angulimala was standing directly behind him and could hear everything that was being said. The Buddha asked Prasenajit, "If Angulimala wished to repent all his mistakes, take vows to renounce killing, and practice loving-kindness and compassion as a monk, would you still want to capture and kill him?"

The king said, "In that case, my Lord, I would not arrest him. If he really can do that, if he can become a gentle monk and practice the mindfulness trainings, then I vow not to arrest and execute him. Instead I will offer him clothing, food, a bed, and medicine." These were the four requisites of a monk in the Buddha's time, given as offerings to monastics by laypeople.

After the king spoke, the Buddha stepped aside and pointed to the monk behind him, "Here is Angulimala."

At first the king was startled and afraid, but through practicing mindful breathing he recognized that he was safe with the Buddha. He turned to Angulimala and asked him, "Bhikshu, what is your name? Where do you come from?"

After Angulimala answered King Prasenajit's questions in a very gentle voice, the king was convinced. He said, "I am ready and eager to offer you the four requisites."

Angulimala replied, "Majesty, I have everything I need, thank you

EARTH-HOLDER AND EARTH-STORE 155

very much for your concern." He spoke in a very gentle and kind way.

Then the king turned to the Buddha and exclaimed, "Wonderful, Lord, wonderful! What you have done no one of us could do, not even an army could do. Your non-fear, gentleness, and compassion have won over Angulimala. You have done the most difficult thing. Your power of transformation and healing is very great. Beloved teacher, I thank you for what you have done to keep peace in the city and in this country."

When he became a monk, Angulimala received the new Dharma name Ahimsa (nonviolence). This shows that it is possible even for someone who has committed very serious crimes and fallen far into the realm of hell to completely transform, and his story can inspire those of you who wish to become a friend of Earth-Store Bodhisattva. As you travel about in the realm of suffering you will encounter many Angulimalas, because they are still here all around us. They need the energy, patience, and steadfastness of this bodhisattva to help them transform their suffering, to help them choose the path of compassion. Those who work in prisons, organizing days of mindfulness to help prisoners learn the path of mindfulness and compassion, embody the action of this bodhisattva. In a prison, in a juvenile detention center, or in a mental health or addiction treatment facility, you will surely meet Angulimala. If you follow the Buddha's example and know how to practice like Earth-Store Bodhisattva, you'll be able to help just as the Buddha did.

❧ TWENTY-SIX

Dharani

T<small>HE TITLE</small> of Chapter Twenty-Six of the *Lotus Sutra*, "Dharani," means "holding fast to." Dharanis are words or phrases that hold great powers of insight and transformation. Just by reciting a dharani mindfully, often repeated three times, we invoke the power of the syllables, the sacred sounds that are produced when our body, speech, and mind are in harmony, unified, in a state of samadhi. With the energy of samadhi, the sound of a dharani can in and of itself bring about transformation.

The practice of reciting dharanis aims at reestablishing communication and understanding with the great beings, the Buddhas and bodhisattvas, in order to receive their spiritual energy. We do not walk the spiritual path alone; we walk in the footsteps of our teachers, friends, fellow practitioners, and all those who have practiced before us, our spiritual ancestors. So the practice of the dharanis is a Dharma door that opens up and allows us to receive the energy of those who support us in our practice.

Though this practice may sound rather strange, it is not difficult to understand. When a Dharma teacher offers a teaching while dwelling in samadhi with purified body, speech, and mind, that power of concentration produces a great source of energy. Those who hear and receive the teaching while in a state of samadhi, dwelling in concentration, will be able to receive that wonderful source of energy, just as if an electric current were to pass between teacher and student. It is the same when we hear or read a sutra in this way—through the sound of the words themselves we receive a kind of powerful spiritual energy and we will be transformed straight away. Listening here does not mean in the ordinary distracted way. When our body, speech, and mind are not in harmony, unified in concentration, if there is anxiety or sadness in our heart and we are only half-listening, then even though we may hear the words being spoken we will not be able to receive the energy of the transmission.

The Buddhas and bodhisattvas have great powers of concentration. When these beings dwell in great samadhi, full of the energy of understanding and compassion, the words they speak or the sounds they produce become dharanis. Any sound, any word—even a single phrase or verse from a sutra, such as the *Lotus Sutra* or the *Heart Sutra*—that is produced in a state of great concentration has the power to transform. For example, the *Heart Sutra* says:

> *The bodhisattva Avalokita*
> *while moving in the deep course of perfect understanding*
> *shed light on the Five Skandhas and found them equally empty.*
> *After this penetration, he overcame ill-being.*[17]

Within Avalokiteshvara there is a great force of wisdom and compassion, and so the words about to be spoken by the bodhisattva are dharanis, produced from his deep insight and great spiritual energy.

> *Listen Shariputra*
> *All dharmas are marked with emptiness,*
> *they are neither produced nor destroyed,*
> *neither defiled nor immaculate,*
> *neither increasing nor decreasing.*

And through this insight, we come to know that:

> *The perfect understanding is the highest mantra,*
> *the unequaled mantra, the destroyer of ill-being,*
> *the incorruptible truth.*

The entire *Heart Sutra* is a dharani, produced by Avalokiteshvara Bodhisattva. Each time we chant this sutra with our body, speech, and mind in harmony we receive the energy of wisdom and compassion of this great bodhisattva. But if we recite it in a rote way, as if we are singing a popular song, we are not able to receive anything. We just drift up and down on the waves of sound without ever becoming immersed.

The chapter on dharani in the *Lotus Sutra* serves to remind us that the Buddhas and bodhisattvas are always present with us whenever we wholeheartedly hear and practice the teachings. They are always producing energy to support us in our practice. The dharanis act as a kind of bridge, a conduit of communication, a way of holding fast to the Buddhas and bodhisattvas and receiving the support of their great spiritual energy.

Dharani is also a tool of transformation. For instance, when we offer food to the hungry ghosts, the ceremony always begins with a dharani for the hungry ghosts, to help increase the size of their throats so that they can receive our offerings. In classical Buddhist literature, hungry ghosts are described as having a big belly but a very tiny throat—so even though they are always very hungry they are never able to take in enough nourishment. There are many kinds of hungry ghost that need our help to transform their suffering. They are hungry for love and understanding but because they are so suspicious, because their hearts are not open enough, they cannot receive our love and compassion. So we offer a dharani that has the power to restore the throats of the hungry ghosts to normal size, to open their hearts, so that they can absorb what is offered to satisfy their great hunger.

There is also a dharani to help bring in as many hungry ghosts as possible, so that they can be nourished by the offerings, and another dharani called "untying the injustice." All the hungry ghosts bear great injustices in themselves and that is why they have become hungry ghosts. Many of us are also victims of injustice, and if there is no compassion and understanding there is no way we can undo the knot of injustice within ourselves and become free. We still continue to suffer if no one can help us undo the knot of injustice in our heart.

Dharani is a means of helping the hungry ghosts. The Sangha is another way. Many hungry ghosts are prevented from coming into contact with those who could help them, because their situation is not an environment where transformation and healing is possible. There are so many hungry ghosts in the world. Many of them are caught in their situation and have no opportunity to experience the kind of safe, calm, stable space that will allow them to get in touch with what is nourishing and healing. So first of all, we invite them to come to us, to the community. We begin with a dharani of universal invitation to all the hungry ghosts so that they might have a chance to experience the healing environment of the Sangha. Otherwise they will be hungry ghosts all their lives, wandering aimlessly in suffering, destroying themselves physically and mentally. Those of you who want to serve as a friend of Earth-Store Bodhisattva must do all you can to provide an opportunity and the kind of safe, healing environment for the hungry ghosts in order to help them transform.

Second, we have to open their hearts so they can take in our offerings of food and drink, of the Dharma, love, compassion, and understanding. Third, we practice deep listening to help them feel understood and loved, so that the feeling of being a victim of great injustice they carry will be dispelled. This is very important for the transformation and healing of the hungry ghost so that he or she can really be reborn in the land of bliss.

The Buddha's medicine is made of only two ingredients: Sangha and time. A new plant has to be in the damp soil for a long time before it can send out new roots, and only a plant that is well-rooted in the earth can produce flowers and fruit. A stable, loving, family and community environment is the nurturing soil that allows us to become rooted spiritually. That is why it is so important to establish and cultivate our Sanghas, not only for our own transformation and healing but in order to better help the hungry ghosts among us.[18]

The only chance a hungry ghost has to heal and transform is to become rooted in a family or community. The hungry ghost's family of origin may not have intended to reject him, they may have done it because they lacked mindfulness and skillful communication. But they can have another chance in their spiritual family. If the Sangha is organized in such a way that it manifests a lot of patience and love, that is the best medicine to help heal a hungry ghost and offer him or her a second chance.

Hungry ghosts are driven by the habit energy in themselves. They may want to tear up the new roots, they may not be able to feel peace, they may not be capable of establishing themselves in the here and now. Even if the Sangha is a good environment they may feel the need to leave the community. That is why it is very important for all of us to become aware of the habit energy in ourselves. It is always pushing us to tear up our roots, to play the role of a wandering soul, a hungry ghost. We can become so used to being a hungry ghost that staying in one place becomes very difficult. So we practice mindful breathing and recognize that the habit energy of being a hungry ghost is still very strong in us. We have to stick with the Sangha and learn how to trust and rely on our Dharma brothers and sisters. We have teachers that can show us the way. We have brothers and sisters who are capable of embracing us and helping us in our practice. With enough good practice, the new plant will eventually take root in the soil of the Sangha, and the feelings of alienation and loneliness will disappear. And then the plant can begin to offer up its flowers and fruit.

So our practice is to help the hungry ghost do these three things: to come to us, to open their hearts in order to receive our offerings, and to experience the healing and transformation that is possible through the practice. This process needs the community and it needs time, the two ingredients of the universal medicine. If you can take this medicine every day for a number of years, then you will have a chance to heal. You will become a plant, a tree, deeply rooted in the soil of the Sangha. Happiness and love become possible. And then you can return to help your own family of origin; you can go back to help your church or synagogue, your community and society transform and become places of healing.

Community, the practice of brotherhood and sisterhood, of love and understanding, is also the antidote to the hungry ghost's recourse to drugs, alcohol, or sex. When you suffer, you often look right away for distraction. You try to forget your suffering by indulging in extremes of sense experience, with sex, alcohol, or drugs. But if you have an alternative—the community, the Sangha—you can go for refuge there. This is why Sangha-building is so crucial for our time. We have to build Sangha everywhere so that the many hungry ghosts wandering in the world will have a place of refuge.

All of us who are the friends of Earth-Store Bodhisattva must pool our ideas and energies to help the many hungry ghosts in our family, community, and society. First of all, we are determined not to create any more hungry ghosts. We participate in the work of preventing more hungry ghosts in our roles as parents, politicians, teachers, or businesspeople—we are careful and responsible in our actions and practice mindfulness of compassion and deep looking. This is the first step. The second step is to help the hungry ghosts that are already here. Whether we go out into the world, travel to the hell realms like Earth-Store, or establish a Sangha and invite them to come to us, we become the arms and hands of the bodhisattva in order to help the hungry ghosts.

❧ TWENTY-SEVEN

King Fine Adornment

C HAPTER TWENTY-SEVEN of the *Lotus Sutra*, "The Former Affairs of the King Fine Adornment," was one of the chapters added later to the sutra. It tells of a king named Shubhavyuha (Fine Adornment), who was the previous life of Flower Virtue, one of the bodhisattvas in the *Lotus Sutra* assembly. Two other bodhisattvas in the assembly, Medicine King and Superior Medicine, were, in their previous lives, the sons of King Fine Adornment. Through their practice and understanding of the *Lotus Sutra*, which they heard taught by the Buddha of that place and time, they were able to lead their father to the path of the Buddhadharma. Also present is the bodhisattva Marks of Adornment, who in a former life was called Pure Virtue, and was the wife of King Fine Adornment and the mother of his two sons.

The Buddha introduces these bodhisattvas and speaks of their past lives to convey to the Sangha that the practice of the *Lotus Sutra* can lead to effects beyond compare, and this has the effect of increasing and insuring the assembly's confidence and faith in the practice. This chapter shows us that we have the capacity to take our practice into our families and communities in order to help them become liberated from suffering. We do not practice for ourselves alone but also in order to help others—this is the way of the bodhisattva that is extolled in the *Lotus Sutra*.

When we enter the bodhisattva path, it is natural that parents and immediate family members are the first objects of our practice. We can see this in the example of Shakyamuni Buddha himself, who soon after his enlightenment taught the Dharma to his aunt Mahaprajapati, his former wife, Yashodara, his son, Rahula, and his father, Suddhodana.

In this chapter, the two sons of King Fine Adornment, who in that lifetime were called Pure Store and Pure Eye, were well-practiced in the bodhisattva path, the practice of the six paramitas, and had attained many samadhis. The Buddha of that time and place was called Wisdom Adorned with Flowers by the King of Constellations Sound of Thundercloud. He wished to draw King Fine Adornment to the Dharma. The two sons wanted to hear this Buddha teach the *Lotus Sutra* and asked their mother for permission to attend the assembly. Pure Virtue told her sons that they should first go to their father and, through powers gained through their accomplishment of the practice, cause him to become receptive to the path of the Dharma. We can see from this that the mother had the capacity to understand her children's deepest spiritual aspirations. In the end, the two sons were able to convince their father to come listen to the Buddha teach the sutra, and in this way they helped their parents cross to the other shore of liberation.

The presence of bodhisattvas like Medicine King, Superior Medicine, and Flower Virtue in the *Lotus Sutra* show us that the practice of the path of liberation has the capacity to not only liberate us but can also bring others out of suffering—beginning with our parents and siblings, our immediate family, and ultimately extending to all beings.

In order to better understand this chapter, we have to understand how Mahayana Buddhism became established as a viable religion in China. Chinese society was strongly influenced by the teachings of Confucianism, which especially upheld the importance of filial duty—the duty and reverence of children toward their parents and ancestors. This ideal has been one of the underpinnings of Chinese society and culture from the time of Confucius in the fifth century B.C.E to the present day. Given this cultural context, we can see that the Buddhist ideal of renunciation—leaving one's home and family to become a monk or nun, a seeker of truth—would have been difficult to accept.

Someone who is practicing always has the capacity to return home in order to liberate their family from suffering. No one practices just for himself or herself alone. When Confucianists condemned Buddhism as failing to practice filial piety, the practitioners had to prove the opposite, that in following the path of the Buddha they were also following the path of humanity and filial piety. In the story of bodhi-sattva Quan Am of the Southern Seas (written in Vietnamese Nom script), we have the following verse:

> *The suchness of the Buddha's path is very wonderful,*
> *Our heart is loyal with filial piety*
> *And the first thought we have*
> *Is to look after humanity.*[19]

Filial piety is our aim to be able to liberate from suffering those who are close to us. Our humanity is our aim to be able to rescue all living beings from drifting and sinking in the ocean of suffering.

TWENTY-EIGHT

Universally Worthy

Now we come to Chapter Twenty-Eight, the final chapter of the *Lotus Sutra*, "The Encouragements of the Bodhisattva Universally Worthy," Samantabhadra.[20] This chapter describes the bodhisattva's vow, that at any time and place where there is even one person practicing the *Lotus Sutra*, he will manifest to offer his support. Universally Worthy is the last bodhisattva mentioned in the *Lotus Sutra*, and his role here is to protect and preserve the sutra, to "broadly propagate it and cause it never to perish." However, this brief chapter is not extensive enough to reveal the full dimension of Samantabhadra, who is called the bodhisattva of Great Action. So we can use elements from other sutras, such as the *Avatamsaka Sutra*, in which the great action of Samantabhadra is explicated more fully, to complete the chapter on this bodhisattva in the *Lotus Sutra*.

The great action of Bodhisattva Universally Worthy can be described as a tenfold practice. The first aspect is paying respect to the Buddha. We often show our respect to the Buddha and bodhisattvas by bowing, but it is important to understand that this action is not a kind of propitiation, in which a devotee pays respect to a powerful divine being in order to gain favor. The Buddha does not need us to pay respect to him; it is we who benefit from this practice. When you pay respect to the Buddha you begin to see the path. You start to walk in the direction of goodness. You know that you are a Buddha-to-be—you have the capacity to become enlightened, awakened. You recognize that you have the capacity to love, to accept, to feel joy and to bring joy to others.

When you bow to the Buddha you are really acknowledging your own capacity for Buddhahood. In acknowledging the Buddha, you acknowledge the Buddha nature inherent within you. This practice can help release you from a negative self-image that keeps you from realizing your true nature. If you don't have this kind of confidence, you will not be able to progress very far on the path. When understood and practiced in this way, paying respect to the Buddha is not merely a devotional ritual but is also a wisdom practice.

In the ceremony of transmission of the Fourteen Mindfulness Trainings, we bow to Manjushri, Avalokiteshvara, and Samantabhadra. As we touch our foreheads to the Earth we touch very deeply the qualities these bodhisattvas represent. For instance, Manjushri represents deep understanding. Manjushri can take many forms; some like to visualize him sitting on a blue lion when they bow. But our gesture of respect toward the bodhisattva has nothing to do with his outer form; when we touch our heads to the Earth we are touching the great wisdom of this bodhisattva. When we bow to Manjushri, we have the awareness that when all those who suffer are able to get in touch with his great wisdom they get relief right away. We know that suffering is born of ignorance, and with understanding our fear, anger, and despair vanish. So, bowing deeply to Manjushri, we acknowledge how great and important is the power of understanding that can liberate us from suffering.

Similarly, when we bow and touch the Earth for Avalokiteshvara, we recognize how wonderful love is. Because of love we are able to do so much and care for so many living beings. When we do things out of love we don't feel tired and we get a lot of happiness right away. We don't feel forced to do anything, we are glad to be able to serve as the arms and hands of the Bodhisattva of Compassion. So our practice is to live our daily life in such a way that every moment, every act becomes an act of love.

And when we bow before Samantabhadra, we can see his power of great action in those who act to bring relief, transformation and healing to other living beings on this Earth. Samantabhadra is not just some abstract figure; he is here all around us, in flesh and bone. In our Sanghas there are bodhisattvas who work tirelessly to help others, to bring relief from suffering. Whether you organize a retreat, or cook for the Sangha, or drive someone to the airport, you are acting as an arm of the Buddha, an arm of Bodhisattva Samantabhadra.

When I bow and touch the Earth, I feel deep respect, deep love. I feel very grateful for all those bodhisattvas surrounding me who follow the example of Manjushri, Avalokiteshvara, Samantabhadra, and all the other great bodhisattvas. Looking at the practice of bowing from the outside, we might get the impression that it is a simple devotional ritual or that it is like praying to a god. This is not true. While it is an expression of our respect and admiration for the Buddhas and bodhisattvas, bowing is not merely a practice of devotion. Breathing mindfully and bowing down to touch the Earth, we are in deep connection with the bodhisattvas and with the qualities they represent. Done in this spirit, bowing is actually a practice of meditation. We get in touch with understanding, compassion, and great action, and see all living beings as the object of our awareness and love. So in showing respect to these great bodhisattvas, we are also demonstrating our commitment to practice the bodhisattva path and cultivate the energy of understanding, love, and compassion within ourselves.

The second aspect of Samantabhadra's practice of great action is praising the Tathagatas. Again, the Tathagatas do not need you to praise them. When we chant in praise of the Buddha we get in touch with the qualities of the Tathagatas. Chanting the Four Recollections, we get in touch with the qualities of the Buddha, Dharma, and Sangha:

> *The Noble Teacher in whom I take refuge*
> *Is the One who embodies and reveals*
> *The Ultimate Reality*
> *Is the One who is worthy of all respect and offering*
> *Is the One who is endowed with perfected wisdom*
> *Is the One who is endowed with right understanding and compassionate action*
> *Is the One who happily crossed to the shore of freedom*
> *Is the One who looked deeply to know the world well*
> *Is the highest charioteer training humankind*
> *Teaching gods and humans*
> *The Awakened One, the World-Honored One.*[21]

When we praise the Buddha's great understanding and wisdom we touch those same virtues that are present within ourselves as seeds in our store consciousness. Through the practice we water those good seeds and cause them to grow. So chanting in praise of the Buddha and Tathagatas is not mere devotion either but also a practice of wisdom and energy. Chanting or listening to chants is an especially good practice when we find ourselves inclined to worry, when we feel anxious or fearful. We should do our best to turn our mind away from anxiety and focus it in a more wholesome direction. Chanting mindfully or listening to chanting can help positive mental activity arise in our consciousness. As with the practice of bowing, though, it is important to understand that the practice of chanting and reciting the sutras is not the same as praying in supplication—we are not asking for something to be given us but performing a practice that helps us touch the good seeds we already have within ourselves. Chanting can be done daily, along with sitting practice. It is a real and effective way to water good seeds so that they will strengthen and grow, and for preventing negative seeds from manifesting.

The third aspect of the great action of Samantabhadra is the practice of making offerings to all Buddhas and living beings. This is the practice of giving. You don't have to be wealthy in order to practice giving. You can make an offering of your practice in your daily life. And you don't need to be a fully ordained monk or nun or a Dharma teacher in order to make an offering of your practice. If you know how to walk mindfully, with solidity and joy, dwelling happily in the present moment, if you practice mindfulness in all your actions, if your eyes are full of joy, conviction, and trust in the Dharma, if your smile manifests your joy in the practice, then you will be able to offer the beauty and joy of your daily practice to the Buddhas and to your own family and community. Whether you are a monastic of ten, twenty, or thirty years' practice, a novice who has just been born into the Dharma, or a layperson, your presence, your way of being, is something of great value that you can offer every minute, every hour of the day.

The fourth aspect of Samantabhadra's great action is the practice of Beginning Anew. In this practice, we admit our past actions that have created obstacles and brought suffering to ourselves and to the people around us, and we state our intention to begin anew. Thanks to the practice of Beginning Anew, you can free yourself from the past. The weight of the past will not be able to crush or paralyze you. You acknowledge your mistakes and take responsibility for the suffering your unskillful actions may have caused, and with that fresh awareness and new insight you become a new person right away.

Beginning Anew gives us the chance for a fresh start, puts us back on the path to liberation. This is possible for everyone. Remember Angulimala, who did so many horrible things? He had even killed his own mother, yet with the Buddha's help he was able to start fresh. Aware of his wrongdoings in the past, he made the vow to stop acting in harmful ways and begin his life anew. This practice is very effective. Those who have been addicted to alcohol or drugs can practice Beginning Anew and free themselves from addiction with the support of the Sangha. All of us who have made mistakes in the past can renew ourselves with this wonderful practice.

The fifth aspect of Samantabhadra's great action is rejoicing at others' realization of the Dharma. Rather than being envious of their accomplishments, you feel genuinely happy for them. This quality of true sympathetic joy (*mudita*) is born from our deep understanding of the nature of interbeing—you want people to be happy because you know that their happiness and achievement are also your happiness and achievement. This practice is the most effective way to deal with envy and jealousy. Understanding the interdependent nature of reality, we are able to experience the accomplishment of any positive thing another person or group has achieved as if it were our own.

The sixth aspect is requesting the Buddhas to turn the wheel of the Dharma. We must go to those who have just received enlightenment, who have just been released from their afflictions and suffering, and ask them to help teach others. There is so much suffering in the world. Those who are able to reach the shore of freedom must not be content only to enjoy their own liberation and peace. We have to go to them and ask them to turn the wheel of the Dharma, to share the Dharma and the practice so that all living beings can cross over the ocean of suffering and affliction and reach the shore of freedom.

The seventh practice is asking the Buddha to remain with us longer in the historical dimention. We ask the Buddha to stay with us, not to enter nirvana, the ultimate dimension, right away, because we still need him. Without the Buddha and the teaching of the Dharma, the world will be plunged into darkness again. So we call on the Buddha's great compassion for us and ask him to stay and continue to teach.

The eighth practice is to always follow the Buddha in order to deepen our practice. We have asked the Buddha to stay and continue to teach us, and so we do everything we can to arrange our lives so that we can continue to learn and practice the Dharma. We must not miss such a precious opportunity. We shouldn't just say to ourselves, "Oh, I can always go and study the Dharma anytime. Right now I am very busy at work, I have so many things to do. Next year I will surely be able to arrange things in order to be able to go and learn the practice." This is not the action of Bodhisattva Universally Worthy. The vow of this bodhisattva is that wherever a Buddha appears to teach the Dharma, he will be present in that place to learn more about the practice. The presence of the Buddhadharma is something very precious, so not only do we ask the teacher of the Dharma to stay longer, we also do our best to stay close to our teacher and learn as much as possible in order to be able to continue the work of liberating all beings.

The ninth aspect of the great action of Samantabhadra is to focus our attention on living beings in order to help them. We practice not just to receive the benefit ourselves but to act as the arms and hands of the Buddha to help others. So we get in touch with living beings, we see their suffering, their yearnings, and their desires as our own suffering and yearning. We look upon others as the object of our practice, always being in accord with them, responding to their needs and considering them as our own family, as our father and mother, as the Buddha. We offer food when they are hungry, we provide medicine when they are sick, we take care of them and help them reconcile when they become divided. This is the path of practice of parents, teachers, health care providers, environmentalists, peaceworkers—all those who express through their lives and work the understanding and compassion of the great bodhisattvas. This aspect of practice is based on our understanding that to serve living beings is to serve the Buddha. Everyone is a Buddha-to-be, so helping living beings is the same as serving and helping the Buddha. This is the greatness of the action dimension of Samantabhadra.

Finally, the tenth aspect of Samantabhadra's great action is transferring all the merits of our practice to the realization of enlightenment. This causes our bodhichitta, our aspiration to realize enlightenment for the sake of living beings, to grow moment by moment. In the chapter on "Merit," the *Lotus Sutra*, we learned that through good acts in our previous lives we build up a store of merit. Every act of body, speech, and mind we have made in the direction of good has created a store of positive energy. Now, following Samantabhadra, we gather up and transfer this great store of spiritual energy to the practice that leads to the liberation of all living beings. We vow to become entirely transformed, fully enlightened, together with all beings. We offer all the merit we have created through our practice, now and in the past, though doing good for others, to the ultimate goal—the collective transformation and liberation of all.

PART IV

Opening the Doors of Action

❧ TWENTY-NINE
The Six Paramitas

I N ONE OF THE CHANTS recited by monks and nuns during
the morning service there is the expression, "opening the
door of action." This refers to entering the dimension of action
through the practice of the six paramitas.[1] The six paramitas are called
the doors of action because this practice is the basis of the bodhisattva
path. It is not only Sadaparibhuta, Avalokiteshvara, Samantabhadra,
and the other great bodhisattvas we have met in the pages of the *Lotus
Sutra*, but you, me, and every one of us who can be Buddha's disciple
and friend and serve as a bodhisattva to help bring peace, joy, and stability to the world.

The Sanskrit term "paramita" is usually translated in English as
"perfection," but in Chinese Buddhist literature it is always rendered
as a character that translates literally as "crossing to the other shore."
The six paramitas are very concrete means for us to cross over the sea
of suffering to the shore of freedom from craving, anger, envy, despair,
and delusion. Through cultivating and perfecting these six ways of
being, we can reach the other shore very quickly—it may take only a
few seconds for us to cross over the river of suffering and arrive on the
shore of well-being. We may have thought that it would take many
years of practice in order to get free of the afflictions but if we know
how to cultivate and manifest these six qualities we can cross over right
here and now.

The first paramita, the first door of action, is dana, giving and generosity. The second door of action is shila, the precepts, mindfulness
trainings, and guidelines for ethical behavior. The third door is kshanti,
all-embracing inclusiveness. The fourth door of action is virya, diligence, energy, effort, and steadfastness in the practice. The fifth is

175

dhyana, meditation, the practice of stopping and calming and looking deeply. And the sixth is prajña, wisdom and understanding.

We have already seen these qualities manifested in the bodhisattvas of the *Lotus Sutra*. Never Despising Bodhisattva and Purna exemplify the perfection of inclusiveness. Manjushri is an example of complete realization of great wisdom. Earth-Store Bodhisattva's vow not to rest until all living beings are delivered from the hells of suffering is an example of the perfection of diligence.

All of the great bodhisattvas manifest the qualities of the six paramitas in various ways, and each of these six doors of action exists in interdependence with the others. In any one of these six qualities, you can see the other five. This is the approach that we should always take when we study and practice Buddhism, because the very foundation of Buddhist wisdom is interbeing—the one contains the all.

It is very important that we understand the nature of interbeing of the six paramitas. By practicing shila, the mindfulness trainings, you are also practicing giving. When you know how to live mindfully, you are offering something very meaningful to the world. The practice of inclusiveness is also a practice of giving. When you fully accept people, embrace them, and take care of them, it is a great gift. Through the practice of embracing and caring for others you help bring about more peace and stability in your family and community. The practices of diligence and meditation also bring a lot of joy, stability, transformation, and healing not only to yourself but also to those around you. And the practice of prajña offers the kind of understanding and wisdom that can help all of us cross over the river of suffering to the shore of liberation.

The six paramitas are an essential practice of the bodhisattva path. In order to manifest ourselves in the dimension of action and serve most effectively as the arms and hands of the Buddhas and bodhisattvas in the world, we practice to cultivate and perfect these six qualities within ourselves. The moment we see the presence of all the paramitas in each paramita we will begin to fully realize and truly live the practice.

ॐ THIRTY

Giving

Giving (DANA) is an essential bodhisattva practice. In Chapter Twenty on Avalokiteshvara Bodhisattva, the Universal Gate, we learned about the four skillful means of a bodhisattva, and the first of these is the practice of making offerings—not just of material goods but the gift of the Dharma, the practice that liberates us from suffering, and the ultimate offering of the bodhisattva, the gift of non-fear. So we have to understand giving in this light. Dana-paramita, the perfection of giving, has nothing to do with material wealth. It has to do with generosity and openness, our capacity to embrace others with our compassion and love and, with that spirit, quite naturally we want to give everything we can to help them. So we can see right away that dana-paramita intersects with the practice of kshanti, inclusiveness, and it also has the element of prajña, wisdom, because it is through our understanding of interbeing that generosity and compassion arise. When we truly see ourselves as others and others as ourselves, we naturally want to do everything we can to secure their happiness and well-being, because we know that it is also our own well-being and happiness.

There's a kind of vegetable in Vietnam called *he* (prounounced "hey"). It belongs to the onion family and looks like a scallion, and it is very good in soup. The more you cut the he plants at the base the more they grow. If you don't cut them they won't grow very much, but if you cut them often, right at the base of the stalk, they grow bigger and bigger. This is also true of the practice of dana. If you give and continue to give you become richer and richer all the time, richer in terms of happiness and well-being. This may seem strange but it is always true. The more you give away the things that you value—not just material things but also gifts of time and energy—the greater your store of riches. How is this possible? When you try to hoard things you may end up losing them, but everything you give to help others always remains with you as the foundation of your well-being.

The practice of dana is wonderful, but it must always be done in the spirit of prajña, understanding. The U.S. has always given a lot to other nations—humanitarian aid, financial help, technological resources, and so on. But these things have been given with the intention of winning others over, of coercing the recipients of this aid to align themselves with U.S. goals and ideology. This kind of giving is motivated by national self-interest, by political and economic expediency. So even humanitarian aid that is given with the hidden agenda of winning people over or cementing a political or economic alliance is not real dana, true giving.

True dana is not a trade, a bargaining strategy. In true giving there is no thought of giver and recipient. This is called the "emptiness of giving," where there is no perception of separation between the one who gives and the one who receives. This is the practice of dana done in the spirit of prajña with the understanding of interbeing. You offer help as naturally as you breathe. You don't see yourself as the giver and the other person as the recipient of your generosity who is now beholden to you and must be suitably grateful, respond to your demands, and so on. You don't give in order to make the other person your ally. When you see that people need help you offer and share what you have with no strings attached, no thought of reward.

There is a story of a very rich man who gave 100,000 pieces of gold to a temple. The abbot had called for financial support from the community to build a new meditation hall, and this wealthy landowner had come forward with a large donation. The abbot was offering tea to several guests, among them the wealthy donor, who displayed the gold on a tray on the table. The abbot did not pay much attention to the money; instead he gave an informal Dharma talk to the group about how to practice the mindfulness trainings and so on. He didn't pay attention to the gold because he believed that while it is good for people to contribute, his task was to help people better understand the Dharma and put it into practice. In fact, the offering was accepted only to support the greater goal of furthering the Dharma.

The wealthy donor grew impatient; he wanted the abbot to remark on the gold and thank him in front of the others. So he interrupted the abbot and asked, "Dear abbot, have you counted this? There are 100,000 pieces of gold here." The abbot said gently, "I know," and continued his Dharma talk. A little while later the man interrupted him again, "But, Reverend Abbot, don't you think 100,000 pieces of gold is a lot?" The abbot looked at him and said, "Do you want me to thank you? I think you should thank me, because I have given you an opportunity to make a donation and gain merit."

Helping to create a meditation hall is an offering for everyone, for the continuation of the Dharma, and it had provided the wealthy man an opportunity to make a contribution and gain the merit of having helped further the Dharma. But he had given the money hoping to be publicly acknowledged as a big donor; he expected a reward and praise for his act of giving. Though he donated a large amount of money he did not offer it in the true spirit of dana.

My right hand does a lot of things—it creates calligraphy and writes poems. Nearly all my poems have been written with my right hand because I don't use a typewriter. There was only one time when I wrote a poem on a typewriter. When inspiration came to me, I did not have a pen at hand so I just put an envelope into the typewriter, and at that time my left hand participated. All the rest of my poems were written with my right hand alone, yet my right hand never says to the left hand, "You, you are good for nothing! You don't do calligraphy, you don't write poems. I do all the work, you never do anything!"

The body never discriminates in this way. Don't think that this is because our bodies do not possess any inherent intelligence. While trying to hang a picture on the wall, I held the nail in my left hand and hammered with the right. But instead of hitting the nail I hit a finger on my left hand. That happens from time to time, especially if you are high up on a ladder. Immediately the right hand put down the hammer and reached over to take care of the left hand, very naturally. The feet began to move to look for a bandage. Everything worked together very smoothly. Later the right hand did not say, "Hey, left hand—remember how I helped you? Next time I need something you have to come and help me." Our innately wise bodies do not act in that way. So the wisdom of nondiscrimination is present in us as a living bodily reality. We have to learn how to train our minds to see in this way.

We form one reality. We exist in interbeing with all of life. When we understand this fundamental truth, our acts of giving will be made in the spirit of nondiscrimination. The merit, the spiritual benefit to be gained from the perfected practice of giving cannot be calculated. The practice of dana brings a lot of happiness when we know how to do it in the spirit of interbeing. You give freely, and you are happy, and you continue to give. Many of us already know how to practice this way. We don't have to give 100,000 pieces of gold or even a single piece of gold; instead we can offer a smile or a loving, compassionate gaze. We can give the gift of our calm, concentrated presence to help someone who is fearful or anxious. We can make an offering of our time and energy and work with the homeless, or with those who are prisoners or are addicted to different substances, or to work on helping the environment. We have plenty of gifts to offer; we are far wealthier than we may imagine. We can help secure the happiness of many people even if we don't have a single penny in our pocket.

The practice of dana-paramita is also an effective antidote to anger. The Buddha taught, "When you are angry with someone, try giving something to him or her." The practice is to prepare a gift in advance and keep it ready. Don't wait until you are angry with someone to prepare something, because with anger and hostility in your mind you won't want to give anything to the object of your anger. It does not have to be a material gift; you can offer a poem or a passage from a teaching, or a song or piece of music, a photograph of a beautiful place. Then, when you become angry with someone, remind yourself of the Buddha's advice. As soon as the idea of giving something to that person comes to you, your suffering will lessen. Usually when we are angry we want only to punish but now we practice the opposite and think only of giving something to the other person. Thanks to this practice, our anger begins to subside right away.

We have to learn how to practice giving in this way on the level of our societies and nations. What can one nation offer to another that it perceives to be its enemy? One nation could say: "We want to offer you the opportunity to live in peace, in self-determination. We want your people to have a safe place to live, and to prosper and enjoy security and well-being." When we are motivated by the desire to give, even if we have not yet offered anything yet, just the intention to offer our help and understanding, our willingness to listen and communicate, begins to lessen our own and others' suffering. Practicing dana-paramita causes our anger and hatred to disappear and we cross to the other shore in a single moment.

When communities and nations practice in this way, they prosper and earn the admiration, respect, and acceptance of other communities and nations. If we could learn to practice this way in our dealings with other nations, we would no longer have to guard the entrances of our embassies, we will no longer be afraid of bombings and terrorist attacks. We would not become isolated and consumed by fear. Happiness can never be possible when there is a lot of fear and suspicion in our consciousness. If we can learn how to open the doors of the six paramitas, individually and collectively, then we will all arrive at the shore of freedom, peace, and safety very quickly.

✌ THIRTY-ONE

Precepts

S HILA, THE SECOND PARAMITA, is the clear and simple guidelines for ethical behavior in our everyday life. "I vow to
listen deeply, with compassion to your suffering." That is shila. "I vow
to speak to you with the language of loving-kindness." That is shila. "I
vow to protect and preserve life." That is shila. The Five Mindfulness
Trainings, the basic precepts of Buddhism, are an essential foundation
for the practice of the other paramitas.[2] When you practice shila, when
you display self-discipline and mindfulness in word and deed, you have
a lot of credibility. Because there is harmony between your words and
actions, people have trust and confidence in you, and with the support
of that trust, you are able to bring about much good. In Plum Village,
we present these trainings in a nonsectarian form, with no specifically
Buddhist terminology, because we know that they have universal value.
Elements of these ethical guidelines for living exist in every tradition.
The wording may be different, but the essence is very much the same.

If we know how to apply the Five Mindfulness Trainings, individually, collectively, and internationally, then peace on Earth will become
a reality. The trainings remind us to consume mindfully and refrain
from doing things that can harm our body and mind. They help us
refrain from harming others and from using the kind of language that
causes disharmony and division and brings about suffering. The practice of shila helps secure the safety and well-being of ourselves and
others, and it is a path to greater understanding and compassion.

It would be wonderful if our governments reflected this kind of
intention and incorporated these guidelines for ethical conduct. Everything we do, every sphere of human activity can be directed toward
supporting the conditions for safety and well-being for the entire

nation and the entire planet. When we align ourselves with this path we naturally garner authority and trust, and we are in the position to open any door. When others look at us, they know that ours is a path of peace, of inclusiveness, and they will not hesitate to join us and become our companions on the path..

It does not take a lifetime to perfect the practice of shila-paramita. The very moment we make the determination to live according to these trainings and practices, joy, healing, and transformation become possible right away. Suppose you have trouble with eating—perhaps you often eat more than you actually need, and this has brought you a lot of difficulty and suffering. You can go for refuge in the training concerning eating and other forms of consumption, the Fifth Mindfulness Training.[3] You may start by making the vow not to eat apart from your family or community. The moment you make a vow in the presence of other members of your family or among your community not to eat outside of regular meals, immediately you will feel a great deal of energy and support. Taking refuge in the support of a community allows us to maintain the precepts very easily.

When we practice mindfulness of our actions in the context of a family or spiritual community we receive the help, support, and encouragement of others. But whether or not we live in community, if our daily life is filled with joy and meaningful, wholesome activity, then we do not feel we are living in a vacuum. When people eat habitually, without mindfulness, it is often because they feel empty inside; there is a lot of loneliness and depression in their heart and mind. Chanting, listening to Dharma talks, practicing walking meditation, doing yoga, and engaging in other wholesome activities that bring calm, relaxation, and joy, whether individually or collectively, give a lot of positive energy and then we won't feel the need to overeat or eat compulsively. The practice of shila is a kind of protection for us, to help us stay on a path of wholesomeness and well-being and avoid the kinds of unskillful, unmindful actions that lead to suffering, not only for ourselves but for all those around us.

So we can see that the element of dana is present in the practice of shila. Our practice of the mindfulness trainings is a big gift for our parents, our children, our loved ones and friends, our community, and for the world. Practicing shila means living in a wholesome way, mindfully, expressing our love, concern, and understanding in every thing we do in our daily life, and that is a big gift for everyone around us, for our nation, and for the Earth. You contribute greatly to the stability and well-being of the world by living according to the mindfulness trainings.

The practice of shila is also based on prajña. The mindfulness trainings are not something imposed on us by a god or a teacher but the result of our own awakening. Aware of the destruction that is going on in the world, aware of the damages of consumerism that is laying waste to the world's resources and causing a lot of suffering for many people all over the world, we naturally become motivated to live in such a way as to protect and preserve life. A mindful and ethical way of life arises naturally out of our awakening, understanding, and love. When awakening and love are strong in you, you won't find it difficult to live according to these precepts. You won't have the feeling that you *have* to practice the mindfulness trainings; rather you *enjoy* practicing them. You become a responsible person quite easily and naturally, because wisdom and love have already taken root in you. When we really love, when we really care, when we are really awake and can see into the nature of interbeing, then the practice of shila doesn't require any special effort and will be perfected quite easily and naturally.

Over the years, some Buddhist practice centers in America and Europe have been plunged into crisis over issues of sexual misconduct and abuse of power by leaders. More recently, many scandals concerning sexual abuse of children by Catholic priests have been brought out into the open, with devastating effects on the Catholic community. These kinds of situations can only occur where mindful awareness and understanding are lacking. Such behavior is a violation of the precepts. Sexual relationships between people in a religious community have the power to destroy the lives of many people, especially children. Why would a religious teacher or leader act in this way, violate their holy vows and cause so much harm and suffering to others? The root cause of such harmful actions is a profound lack of understanding and compassion.

A teacher who has truly perfected the practice of the precepts will not find it difficult to refrain from entering into a sexual relationship with one of his or her disciples. This does not mean they don't love their students; on the contrary, it is precisely because they do love their disciples and students that they refrain from such an act. Because I love you and wish to protect you, and want you to succeed on your path of realization, I practice the precepts. Mindfulness of love, awareness, and understanding are the elements that protect us and help us to practice shila perfectly. With love and understanding we don't have to make any effort yet our practice of the precepts will be perfect. Practicing shila with a lot of struggling and effort, with self-recrimination and harshness, is not correct. It is only the presence of understanding and love in ourselves that allows us to make the right choices and practice a mindful and compassionate way of life naturally and effortlessly.

❧ THIRTY-TWO

Inclusiveness

THE SANSKRIT WORD "kshanti" is often translated as "for-bearance," or "endurance," but this does not really convey the true meaning of this paramita. Forbearance implies that you have to suffer a little bit in order to be able to accept something. If we look at the Chinese character for "kshanti," in the lower part is the character for "heart," and in the upper part there is a stroke that looks like a knife, something sharp that is a little bit difficult to handle. This is a graphic expression of its true root meaning, "all-embracing inclusiveness." If our heart is large and open enough we can accept the sharp thing and it will not bother us. Something that seems unpleasant or disturbing only feels that way when our heart is too small. When our heart is large enough we can be very comfortable, we can embrace the sharp, difficult thing without injury. So kshanti is a quality of being that does not bring suffering; in fact, it allows us to escape the kind of suffering we experience when our heart is too small. When our heart is big enough we won't suffer.

The Buddha offers us a very beautiful illustration of this principle. Suppose you have a handful of salt and you pour it into a bowl of water and stir it. Now the water in the bowl is too salty to drink. But if you throw that handful of salt into a river, it will not turn the river salty and people can continue to drink the water. When you are only a bowl of water, you suffer. But when you become a river you don't suffer anymore.

If our heart remains small we may suffer very deeply from all the difficulties we encounter in life—heat, cold, floods, bacteria, sickness, old age, death, stubborn people, cruel people. But through the practice of kshanti we can embrace everything and we won't have to suffer.

A small heart cannot accept too much, it cannot take in and embrace everything, every difficulty that arises. But a heart that is expansive and open can easily accept everything and you no longer have to suffer. Perfecting the practice of kshanti consists of continually making your heart bigger and bigger so that it can accept and embrace everything. That is the power and the miracle of love.

Each of us must ask ourselves, how large is my heart? How can I help my heart grow bigger and bigger every day? The practice of inclusiveness is based on the practice of understanding, compassion, and love. When you practice looking deeply to understand suffering, the nectar of compassion will arise naturally in your heart. Maitri, loving-kindness, and karuna, compassion, can continue to grow indefinitely. So thanks to the practice of looking deeply and understanding, your loving-kindness and compassion grow day by day. And with enough understanding and love you can embrace and accept everything and everyone.

Very often in a conflict we feel that if those on the other side, those who oppose us or believe differently from us, ceased to exist then we would have peace and happiness. So we may be motivated by the desire to annihilate, to destroy the other side, or to remove certain people from our community or society. But looking deeply we will see that just as we have suffered, they have also suffered. If we truly want to live in peace, safety, and security, we must create an opportunity for those on the other side to live this way as well.

If we know how to allow the other side into our heart, if we have that intention, not only do we suffer less right away but we also increase our own chances of peace and security. When we are motivated by the intention to practice inclusiveness, it becomes very easy to ask, "How can we best help you so that you can enjoy safety? Please tell us." We express our concern for their safety, their need to live in peace, to rebuild their country, to strengthen their society. When you are able to approach a situation of conflict in this way it can help transform the situation very quickly. The basis for this transformation, the first thing that must happen, is the change within your own heart. You open your heart to include the other side; you want to give them the opportunity to live in peace, as you wish to live.

Societies and nations that are locked in conflict need to learn the practice of inclusiveness if they really want to find a way to live together in peace. Can our side accept the fact that the other side also needs a place to live and the safety and stability that can guarantee a peaceful and prosperous society? When we look deeply into the situation of those on the other side we see that they are just like us—they also want only to have a place where they can live in safety and peace. Understanding our own suffering and our own hopes can lead to understanding the suffering and hopes of the other group. We know that if the other side does not have peace and safety, then it will not be possible for us to have peace and safety. That is the nature of interbeing. With this insight we'll be able to open our heart and embrace the other side.

ॐ THIRTY-THREE

Diligence

THE NEXT PARAMITA, virya, is very often misinterpreted. Bringing the quality of diligence to our practice does not mean that we have to drive ourselves very hard and suffer a lot. Many people think that to be a diligent practitioner you have to practice sitting meditation for one hour, or two hours, or you have to sit all day until you feel pain all through your body, and you think that this is good. You are able to push yourself hard and so you feel like a hero. You can bear the pain in your mind and body. You have made it. You have survived a retreat.

This is not the practice of virya. You don't have to suffer in order to progress in the practice. True diligence, wholesome energy and effort in our practice, is born from joy. The point of the practice is not to create more suffering but to bring well-being, transformation, and healing. We are not practicing only to achieve some better state in the future but in order to get in touch with the joy and peace that are available right now, in every moment. If you practice with the correct attitude you will feel relief from suffering right away.

When you breathe, sit, walk, and observe mindfully, you concentrate and with that concentration you are able to look deeply and touch the wonders of life that are all around you. The result is immediate. As you breathe in you are able to embrace your pain and sorrow so as to bring relief right away. If you continue to practice in this way, you will continue to feel great relief, transformation, and joy. Mindfulness brings many kinds of results. If the object of your mindfulness is something pleasant, you increase the joy. If the object of mindfulness is pain, you bring relief to it. Mindfulness always carries concentration within itself, and when you live with concentration you will be able to see deeply into the heart of reality.

The teaching on diligence is made clear in the Four Right Efforts.[4] These are four practices that help us avoid creating new situations of suffering and help us transform the suffering we do have. According to Buddhist psychology, our consciousness contains the store consciousness at the base, and the mind consciousness in the upper level. In the store consciousness there are many seeds, both wholesome and unwholesome. These seeds are the result of our past actions and they can either manifest or remain dormant according to how we attend to them.[5]

So the first of the four practices of diligence is not to plant new negative seeds in our consciousness. If the seed of an unwholesome act of body, speech, and mind has not yet been planted in you, don't plant it. For example, if you don't have the seed of enjoying drugs, alcohol, or other things that disturb your mental and physical health and stability, then don't expose yourself to situations where that seed might become planted in your consciousness. That is the first element of diligence, and we must use our intelligence and understanding to practice it.

The second practice of diligence concerns what to do with the negative seeds we already have. This involves arranging your daily life in such a way that these seeds will not have a chance to manifest and grow. We have to practice a way of living that does not water the seeds of anger, despair, and craving in ourselves every day. Creating a sane, healthy environment for ourselves and our children is a big task. We must create communities where we can be in touch with the wonders of life and be surrounded by others who practice mindful living so that the negative seeds in us and in our children will not be watered every day.

For twenty years I have been speaking about the need to create communities of resistance, communities of mindful living that offer an alternative to the unhealthy and wasteful ways of living that so many people are engaged in. We are constantly being exposed to negative things in society, assaulted day and night by what we see and what we hear. The negative seeds in us are watered every day and they continue to grow. That is why it is so important to reflect on how to organize our families and communities so that we can be protected from the constant invasion and assault of craving, hostility, and delusion. If we do not protect ourselves from the influence of these poisons we will not be able to help and protect others, including our own children and loved ones.

The second practice includes not allowing the negative seeds in us to be watered and to manifest on the level of our mind consciousness. When they manifest themselves like that, their base is strengthened. A seed that is simply maintained in our store consciousness for a long time will gradually become less powerful. But if it has a chance to manifest in our mind consciousness then it continues to grow from the base. So we must diligently practice not to water the negative seeds of despair, anger, craving, and so on.

The third practice of diligence is to water the positive seeds that we already have in our store consciousness. If these good seeds have not yet manifested, we practice to help them to manifest. If they have already have manifested we try to maintain them as long as possible in our mind consciousness. Again, our environment is very important. When we surround ourselves with good friends, good Dharma brothers and sisters, they can help us get in touch with the positive seeds in our store consciousness, and the positive seeds are watered and able to manifest.

How does this work? Suppose you begin to feel angry; instead of becoming consumed by that emotion, you listen to a Dharma talk or you talk to one of your Dharma brothers or sisters. That can stop the seed of anger from manifesting fully and then you can replace it with the manifestation of loving-kindness. It is like changing channels on a television. If you find the right channel you receive a good image, and every time you see a negative image on the screen you change the channel. Our consciousness also works like this. There are thousands of channels in our consciousness and it's up to us to choose the right channel, the channel of the Buddha and bodhisattvas, instead of the channel of the hungry ghosts.

The fourth practice of diligence is to maintain the positive seeds that have manifested so that they continue to strengthen and grow. The longer we are able to hold these positive seeds in our mind consciousness, the stronger they will grow at the base, in our store consciousness. They are like wonderful guests that we want to host as long as possible in our mind consciousness so that they have the opportunity to grow at the base. This is called transformation at the base. And as the wholesome seeds continue to grow, the unwholesome seeds continue to weaken.

Diligence requires understanding and the other paramitas in order to be practiced in the best, most effective way. The practice of shila, the mindfulness trainings, is a very good method for creating a healthy environment for ourselves, our family, and our community so we can practice diligence. We can get a lot of joy from practicing the other paramitas, yet many of us believe that virya-paramita has to be difficult. So we practice very hard, believing that this is the best, most rigorous kind of practice, but our practice is joyless and we suffer. Practicing diligence in this way cannot bring good results no matter how hard we work. This is why our practice must be informed by prajña, understanding. With the element of understanding your practice will bring a lot of relief and joy to you right away, it will be healing and transformative, and that transformation and healing will encourage you to be more and more diligent in your practice.

✌ THIRTY-FOUR

Meditation

DHYANA, meditation, is the practice of calming, concentrating, and looking deeply. Meditation should be understood first of all as the cultivation of samadhi, meditative awareness. Then when we take teachings such as the Three Dharma Seals— impermanence, non-self, and nirvana—as the object of our concentration, they become real insights into our lived experience, not just ideas or concepts.

The core Buddhist teaching of impermanence tells us that all things arise and pass away, according to their causes and conditions. Nothing lasts forever; nothing is a permanent, unchanging thing unto itself. Many practitioners think that they understand the teaching of impermanence perfectly but they do not really believe in it. We have a strong tendency to believe that we will remain the same person forever, and that our loved ones will also remain the same forever, but this is a kind of delusion that prevents us from living in a more mindful and compassionate way. If we believe that everyone and everything we love will always be there, we have little concern to take care of them, to treasure them deeply right here and now. When we lose something or someone we love, we suffer. Yet when that thing or person was still present in our lives we may not have treasured it, we didn't fully appreciate him or her, because we lacked the insight of impermanence. It's very important to make the insight of impermanence the object of our meditative awareness, because this insight is an essential element of love and compassion.

When we are able to look at ourselves and our loved ones in the light of impermanence, we know what to do right now to bring joy to ourselves and others, because tomorrow may be too late. When we

193

become angry with someone, it is because we lack the insight of impermanence and the insight of non-self. We may think that happiness is an individual matter. But when we look deeply into the nature of interbeing, we see clearly that if the other person suffers there is no way we can be truly happy. When we are angry with someone, we suffer our own anger. When you can do something to make another person happy, to bring a smile to his or her face, you also feel joy right away. Our happiness is made of others' happiness, and our suffering is also made of others' suffering. So the understanding of impermanence, non-self, and interbeing inspires us to do everything we can to relieve suffering and bring joy and happiness in our daily life.

The insight of impermanence is not just an intellectual understanding. There is a big difference between the idea of impermanence and the insight of impermanence. The teaching of impermanence is offered only so that we can realize the insight of impermanence. We must know how to make use of this teaching in an intelligent way in order to get the insight. We must take care not to get caught in dogma, in a conceptual understanding of impermanence, non-self, and nirvana. We have to be able to transform what we learn into real insight and keep this insight alive in our daily life.

The insight of impermanence can illuminate every moment of your life. When I strike a match, flame is produced. It's because of the match that the flame can manifest but as soon as the flame manifests it begins to consume the match. The notion of impermanence is like the match; the insight of impermanence is the flame. Once we have received the insight we no longer need to hold on to the notion. Insight replaces our limited conceptual understanding.

We can not liberate ourselves with a mere notion. We can talk about it all we want, but without real insight there will be no change in our lives and in the world. If you know how to practice looking deeply to transform your notion of impermanence and non-self into the flame of real insight, that insight will illuminate your daily life, moment to moment. You will know what to do and what not to do in order to bring well-being and happiness to yourself and others.

∾ THIRTY-FIVE

Wisdom

T HE *Prajñaparamita Sutra* describes the perfection of wisdom, prajña-paramita, as "the wings of a bird that can carry you very far." It is the foundation and the key to the realization of all the paramitas. With this kind of understanding we can practice giving, mindfulness, inclusiveness, diligence, and meditation perfectly. Without prajña-paramita the perfection of the other paramitas is impossible—without wings you cannot go far.

In the last chapter we learned how understanding is present in the practice of meditation. We practice dhyana in order to produce the insight of impermanence and of non-self in our daily life. Impermanence and non-self belong to the historical dimension of reality. Everything is impermanent, everything is without a separate existence. Yet it is only when we touch deeply impermanence and non-self, the characteristics of the historical dimension, that we are able to touch the ultimate dimension, nirvana. So when our practice of dhyana is informed by prajña we are able to touch nirvana right within impermanence and non-self. We realize that there is no separation between the historical and ultimate dimensions. This is prajñaparamita.

The practice of inclusiveness means you have the capacity to accept and embrace everything—including sickness, old age, and death. When you bring the element of prajña to your daily life, keeping the insight of impermanence and non-self alive in every moment, you are able to touch the ultimate ground of no birth and no death. That is touching nirvana. And when you are able to touch the ultimate dimension, it becomes very easy to accept and embrace birth and death, manifestation and non-manifestation. It is impossible to practice perfect inclusiveness without prajña, insight into the ultimate dimension, nirvana. A child does not become sad when a particular arrangement of colors and patterns in the kaleidoscope disappears, because she knows that another wonderful manifestation will appear. Impermanence and non-self are simply turns of the kaleidoscope, where one manifestation seamlessly gives way to another.

When we can bring prajña-paramita into our practice of the other paramitas, then we can truly say that we have perfected them. We have taken the teachings of the *Lotus Sutra*'s bodhisattva's into our daily life. The perfection of dana is to give completely free of the notion that there is any separation between giver, recipient, and gift. This is a very deep practice, and prajña is its foundation. Perfect giving, dana-paramita, can only happen on the ground of perfect understanding, prajña-paramita.

We can bring the element of prajña to any practice, such as bowing. The Buddhist tradition has this very beautiful gatha: "The one who bows and the one who is bowed to, both of us are perfectly empty." How can we understand this? We know that the Buddha is made of non-Buddha elements, including ourselves. And you are made of non-you elements, including the element of the Buddha. This insight into our nature of emptiness, and the nature of emptiness of the Buddha, is prajña. With this understanding we can remove the boundary between the one who bows and the one who is bowed to. When you bow to the one that is the image of perfection, the absolute, the Buddha, you see yourself reflected there and you are able to recognize that ultimate perfection in yourself. There is no separation between you and the object of your reverence, and you experience a deep connection to the Buddha within. If you remain entirely yourself and Buddha remains entirely himself or herself, deep contact and perfect communication between you will not be possible.

Understanding the emptiness of things in this way is prajña-paramita, perfect wisdom, and it is the basis of our practice of bowing or of any other practice we undertake. When we have realized perfect understanding in our practice of the paramitas, then we will find that we are already free. Understanding that birth and death are just a game, a hide-and-seek game between the historical and the ultimate dimensions, we are completely free of fear. Through the *Lotus Sutra*, we see the possibility of perfect understanding. We can enter the Great Vehicle of the bodhisattvas and together with all living beings cross over to the shore of liberation.

❧ Conclusion

T HE *Lotus Sutra* is not a scholarly work for specialists, but a practical guide for living our lives here and now. The heart of the *Lotus Sutra* teaching, the bodhisattva way of the Great Vehicle, is this: We are all bodhisattvas. We can use the sutra, and the insight it gives us into the six paramitas, in our life every day. When we study the sutra we do not study it just for ourselves but for the benefit of all people. When we cook a meal, wash a saucepan, sweep the Dharma hall, or go to work, we are not just doing these things for our own benefit. Taking even one step in a mindful way can help create the energy of mindfulness that will benefit all beings of the Earth. We practice not only to transform ourselves but to help others transform as well, because we know that we inter-are with all of life. Following the practice of the great bodhisattvas, we cultivate a heart of love and compassion, concentration and insight, and in this way all our actions of body, speech, and mind will be beneficial for all living beings.

❧ Notes

Notes to the Introduction

1 Leon Hurvitz, *Scripture of the Lotus Blossom of the Fine Dharma* (*The Lotus Sutra*), translated from the Chinese of Kumarajiva (New York: Columbia University Press, 1976). All quotes from the *Lotus Sutra* in this book, unless otherwise noted, are from this edition.

2 Mahayana ("Great Vehicle") is the name of a major development of the Buddhist tradition that took place around the first century B.C.E to the first century C.E. To distinguish its teachings from those of the early Buddhist tradition, Mahayanists referred to the early Buddhist teachings, somewhat derogatorily, as the Hinayana ("Small Vehicle").

3 There are several clues that tell us this. The first Buddhist master to quote from the *Lotus Sutra* was the great Mahayana master Nagarjuna, who lived at the end of the second century C.E. He was the author of the *Mahaprajna-paramita-shastra* (*The Commentary on the Great Transcendant Understanding*) and founder of the Madhyamaka ("Middle Way") school.

   From the internal evidence of the *Lotus Sutra* itself, we can see that it must have been composed after other Mahayana sutras such as the *Vimalakirtinird-esha*. The *Vimalakirtinirdesha* presents one of the most powerful critiques of the Hinayana, while the *Lotus Sutra* aims to reconcile the teachings of the two vehicles—the Hinayana and the Mahayana. Thus the *Lotus Sutra* must have appeared after such Mahayana texts as the *Vimalakirtinirdesha*. See the translation by Robert A. F. Thurman, *The Holy Teaching of Vimalakirti* (University Park, PA, and London: Pennsylvania University Press, 1976).

4 This way of organizing the sutra was the contribution of the T'ien-t'ai school in China (known as the Tendai school in Japan), which specialized in the study of the *Lotus Sutra*. The T'ien-t'ai scholars made many deductions about the ideas expressed in the sutra, and established the theory and practice of their school of Buddhism on its teachings. This school was a very important one in China, and influenced the development of other major schools of Mahayana Buddhism in China and Japan, including the Pure Land and Ch'an (Zen)

traditions. The teachings of the *Lotus Sutra* were very influential in the development of later Mahayana thought and practice.

5   The "ten directions" are the four cardinal directions of north, south, east, and
west; the four intermediary directions of northeast, southeast, northwest, and
southwest; plus the zenith and nadir—thus everywhere, in every direction.

Notes to Chapter One

1   Jainism was founded by a contemporary of Shakyamuni, Mahavira, and it too
rejected the authority of the Vedas, the foundational texts of Brahmanism (the
precursor of Hinduism). It is one of the very few of the many religious sects
that arose in this period to have survived to the present day in India.

2   Original Buddhism or "Source" Buddhism describes the earliest period of the
Buddha's teachings, which were initially transmitted orally for about a hundred
years after his lifetime, then collected and recorded in the Pali Canon in the
fourth century B.C.E. These teachings form the basis of the Hinayana, more
properly known as the Theravada ("Way of the Elders"). This is the primary
form of Buddhism practiced in Sri Lanka, Burma, Thailand, Cambodia, and
Laos, and parts of southern Vietnam. Mahayana Buddhism is the primary form
practiced in most of Vietnam, China, Korea, and Japan, while Tibetan Buddhism is a highly specialized form of Buddhism called Vajrayana that incor-
porates elements of the Hinayana, Mahayana, and Tantric traditions.

3   The Theravada is still represented in Sri Lanka today in one of its subdivisions
known as the Tamrasatiya school. In the past the Theravada school was also
represented in Kashmir in the form of another subdivision known as the Sarvastivada. It lasted for about one thousand years (300 B.C.E - 700 C.E.) and the
three collections of this school were taken to China where they were translated
into Chinese and are extant today. We should remember that these two schools
do not represent Original Buddhism but the Schools' Buddhism that arose
after the lifetime of Sakyamuni Buddha. The collections of the Tamrasatiya
school are known as the Southern Transmission and those of the Sarvastivada
as the Northern Transmission. Although it is sometimes felt that because of its
conservatism the Theravada school is closer to Original Buddhism than is the
Mahasangika school, this is not so. Because of its way of transmission, preser-
vation and exposition of the Buddha's teachings, the Theravada school is not
the same as Original Buddhism.

4   The sutra and vinaya collections are known as the Sutra pitaka (Basket of Ser-
mons or Talks of the Buddha) and Vinaya pitaka (Basket of Mindfulness Trainings). For more on the early development of Buddhism and the doctrinal

schisms between the various schools, see Edward Conze, *Buddhist Thought in India* (Ann Arbor, MI: University of Michigan Press, 1967).

5 The Abhidharma ("Super Dharma"), a primary text of Source Buddhism, is part of the Tipitaka (Sanskrit: Tripitaka), the three divisions of the Pali Canon, along with the Sutta-pitaka (Sanskrit: Sutra-pitaka), the original discourses of the Buddha; and the Vinaya-pitaka, the monastic code.

6 For more on pratityasamutpada, see Chapter 27, "The Twelve Links of Interdependent Co-Arising," in *The Heart of the Buddha's Teaching* (Berkeley, CA: Parallax Press, 1998), pp. 206–232.

7 The Five Mindfulness Trainings are the basic precepts undertaken by all Buddhists: not to kill; not to steal; not to engage in unwholesome sexual activity; not to use false speech; and not to consume intoxicants. For more on these basic precepts, see Chapter 13, "Right Action," in *The Heart of the Buddha's Teaching*, pp. 86–90. The *Pratimoksha* is a part of the Vinaya-pitaka that contains the 250 rules of conduct for monks and the 348 rules of conduct for nuns.

8 Founded by Thich Nhat Hanh in 1966 during the Vietnam War with the aim of applying Buddhism in modern life, the Order of Interbeing (Tiep Hien) has an international monastic and lay membership. For more about the Order including its charter, precepts and a brief history see Thich Nhat Hanh *Interbeing* (Berkeley, CA: Parallax Press, 1997).

9 Hurvitz, Chapter 23, "The Former Affairs of the Bodhisattva Medicine King," *Scripture of the Lotus Blossom of the Fine Dharma*, p. 298.

10 Hurvitz, Chapter 10, "Preachers of Dharma," *Scripture of the Lotus Blossom of the Fine Dharma*, pp. 177–178.

11 *William Wordsworth* (Oxford University Press, 1990), pp.138–140.

12 Many extant Sanskrit versions of the *Lotus Sutra* have been found in Nepal, Kashmir, and Central Asia. Versions have also been found in Tibet, and recently a version was found in Khotan (present-day western China) which was a major Buddhist center in Central Asia until the middle of the ninth century.

13 Tradition holds that there were seventeen different Chinese versions of the *Lotus Sutra*, some complete and others not. Today there remain only three complete versions in the Chinese canon, and the clearest, most readable version is the translation by the Chinese monk-scholar Kumarajiva (344–413 C.E.).

14 It was necessary for some time to pass before people began to see and criticize the shortcomings in the sutra that resulted in the addition of new chapters. The first chapters of the *Lotus Sutra* offer the teaching that all living beings have the capacity to become Buddha, which means that all kinds of

practitioners, including shravakas, pratyekabuddhas, and bodhisattvas, have the capacity for Buddhahood. This is the essential teaching of the *Lotus Sutra*. However, it is striking that not until Chapter Twenty-Two is there mention of women becoming Buddhas. So later scholars added Chapter Thirteen, in which the Buddha's aunt, Mahaprajapati Gotami, and his former wife, Yashodhara, the mother of Rahula, are also predicted to become Buddhas.

Chapter Twelve, on the Buddha's cousin Devadatta, was also added later. Devadatta caused the Buddha a lot of trouble, and in principle he should not be able to become enlightened due to the extremely negative karma he had created by harming the Buddha. Nevertheless, the wide embrace of the *Lotus Sutra* includes *all* living beings. The sutra confirms that we all have Buddha nature, the capacity to become fully awakened. So there had to be a new chapter about Devadatta in which he is also predicted to become a Buddha in the future. Only through this gradual process of the development of the sutra in different stages and the later addition of new chapters is the principal teaching of the *Lotus Sutra* wholly realized.

15 The *Ramayana* is the saga of Prince Rama, an incarnation of the Hindu god Vishnu. The *Mahabharata* tells the story of an epic battle between two families, symbolic of the triumph of good over evil. The *Bhagavad Gita* is part of the *Mahabharata*. The two most important Hindu epics, they are still performed in various theatrical forms in South and Southeast Asia today.

Notes to Part One

1 Nagas (snakes or dragons), kinnaras (celestial singers), ghandharvas (celestial musicians), asuras (demigods), and garudas (mythical giant birds) are various types of mythical beings originally from Indian folklore. They often appear in Buddhist sutras as part of the assembly gathered to hear a teaching, representing the cosmic reach of the Buddha's teaching.

2 A protuberance found on the crown of the head of any Buddha.

3 The lokadhatu, the world of men. Saha is Sanskrit for suffrance, endurance.

4 Hurvitz, p.28.

5 These nine types of teachings are listed in the *Lotus Sutra*. In addition there are three other types: future predictions (*vyakarana*), inspired sayings (*udana*), and extensive teachings (*vaipulya*), in the classical designation of the twelve divisions of the Buddhist teachings.

6 The term "one vehicle" first appears in the Sutra on the Four Establishments of Mindfulness (Satipatthana Sutta, Majjhima Nikaya 10). See *Transformation*

and Healing: Sutra on the Four Establishments of Mindfulness (Berkeley, CA: Parallax Press, 1990). In this sutra, the practice of mindfulness is described as the "one way in," or the "one vehicle" that leads to liberation. So this idea was already present in the early Buddhist tradition and is not wholly new to the Mahayana, though it takes on a much greater significance in the *Lotus Sutra.*

7 Bodhichitta means literally "mind (*chitta*) of enlightenment (bodhi)." Generating the aspiration to attain enlightenment, not for one's own liberation only but in order to help all other beings to liberation, is the first step on the path of the bodhisattva.

8 The "Buddha vehicle" (*buddhayana*) is another name for the One Vehicle. The term "bodhisattvayana" is used to distinguish the bodhisattva path from the shravakayana and the pratyekabuddhayana (which are often referred to as the "two vehicles"). The Buddha vehicle embraces all three vehicles.

9 Hurvitz, p. 34.

10 Hurvitz, p.47.

11 From a psychological point of view, this section describes the state of mind of some people at the time when the *Lotus Sutra* appeared, but it also describes a view still held by some in our own time.

12 Hurvitz, p.53.

13 Hurvitz, p.74.

14 The Three Dharma Seals are impermanence, non-self, and nirvana. They are the mark of an authentic Buddhist teaching. For a detailed explanation, see Thich Nhat Hanh, *The Heart of the Buddha's Teaching* (Berkeley, CA: Parallax Press, 1998) pp. 122–135.

15 Hurvitz, p.75.

16 In many Mahayana sutras, the term "Dharma doors" appears, often said to number 84,000, a symbolic number that represents the incalculable various teachings through which the Buddhadharma may be entered.

17 Hurvitz, p.97-98.

18 Prophecy or prediction teachings (vyakarana) are one of the twelve divisions of the Buddhist teachings, nine of which, including parables (aupamya), are listed in Chapter Two of the *Lotus Sutra.*

19 A *yojana* is an ancient Indian measurement of distance, roughly fifteen miles, based on the distance that can be covered by foot in one day.

20 In my book *Old Path, White Clouds* (Berkeley, CA: Parallax Press, 1991), it was my intention to help the Buddha reveal himself as a human being again so that we can be in touch with him as a person like ourselves.

21 For a complete description of the Buddha's life story, see *Old Path, White Clouds.* Chapter Five, "A Bowl of Milk," recounts the moment when Siddhartha, near death from his years of ascetic practice, discovered the "middle way" between extremes of indulgence and asceticism.

22 In the Pali Canon the five grave offenses are: 1) patricide, 2) matricide, 3) killing an arhat, 4) causing blood to flow from the body of a Buddha, and 5) causing a schism in the Sangha. According to the Hinayana, those who commit any of these deeds are consigned to hell, without any possibility of transformation that would lead to a more favorable rebirth in the future.

23 Devadatta proposed five ascetic practices: monks should dwell in the forest and never sleep in villages or towns; monks should not live in buildings or huts but should live outside under the trees; monks should not accept invitations to eat in laypeople's homes but should return to the forest with their almsfood; monks should not accept *sanghati* robes offered by laypeople but should sew their own robes out of scraps of cloth they had scavenged; monks should eat only vegetarian food.

24 According to the way of thinking at the time, people believed that it was not possible to attain Buddhahood in the body of a woman; you had first to be reborn in a male body in order to be able to perform the bodhisattva practices and become a Buddha. The next chapter of the sutra, added later, affirms that anyone, man or woman, can become a Buddha.

25 Hurvitz, p.204.

26 It was not until about 100 B.C.E that sutras began to be written down on palm leaves and gathered together.

27 Of the later Mahayana schools founded on the *Lotus Sutra*, the Nichiren Shoshu school, founded by the Thirteenth-century Japanese monk Nichiren, is centered on the practice of reciting the name of the sutra in the mantra *Namu Myoho Renge Kyo.*

Notes to Part Two

1 The three bodies (*trikaya*) of the Buddha are the "transformation body" or "manifestation body" (*nirmanakaya*); the "body of enjoyment" (*sambhogakaya*); and the Dharma body (dharmakaya).

2 The *Vajracchedikaprajñaparamita –sutra* (*Diamond Sutra*) mentions four signs— self, person, living being, and life span—illusory appearances of reality to which we become attached. See Thich Nhat Hanh, *The Diamond That Cuts through Illusion: Commentaries on the Prajñaparamita Diamond Sutra* (Berkeley, CA: Parallax Press, 1992).

3 "Signlesseness" (*animitta*) is a clarified perception of reality that is able to see past the outer signs, marks, or images (*lakshana*) of reality that ordinary perception takes to be inherently real—i.e., as possessing solid and permanent selfhood. For more on this teaching, see *The Heart of the Buddha's Teaching*, pp. 138–142.

4 Hurvitz, p.193.

5 Hurvitz, p.236.

6 "Tathagata," literally, "one who goes to or comes from suchness (*tatha*)," is a common epithet for a Buddha, an awakened one who has seen into the true nature, or suchness, of reality.

7 "Nayutas" and "asamkhyeyas" are Sanskrit terms that describe increasingly greater, incalculable, infinite numbers of things. A kalpa is an infinitely vast unit of time, an eon.

8 Hurvitz, p.238.

9 From "Butterflies Over the Golden Mustard Fields" in Thich Nhat Hanh, *Call Me By My True Names* (Berkeley, CA: Parallax Press, 1999) p. 76.

10 The teachings on the eight levels of consciousness—from the store consciousness to the sense consciousnesses— are the main subject of the Manifestation Only school of Buddhism, also known as Consciousness Only (Vijñaptimatra) or Yogachara, founded in the fourth to fifth centuries by the Indian masters Vasubandhu and Asanga. For a detailed explication of Vasubandhu's foundational work on the levels and functioning of consciousness, see Thich Nhat Hanh, *Transformation at the Base: Fifty Verses on the Nature of Consciousness* (Berkeley, CA: Parallax Press, 2001).

11 A "long, broad tongue" is one of the thirty-two auspicious marks (*dvatrimshad-vara-lakshana*), or physical characteristics, that distinguish a Buddha and other great beings. Among the other marks are the ushnisha, a cone-shaped protuberance on the head, and the *urna*, a tuft of hair between the eyebrows.

12 Anuttara samyak sambodhi ("perfect, universal enlightenment") is the highest, complete enlightenment of a Buddha.

13 Thich Nhat Hanh, *Miracle of Mindfulness* (Boston, MA: Beacon Press, 1987).

Notes to Part Three

1 Hurvitz, *Scripture of the Lotus Blossom of the Fine Dharma*, p. 283.

2 Quoted from "Awakening Words of Master Quy Son," in Thich Nhat Hanh, *Stepping Into Freedom* (Berkeley, CA: Parallax Press, 1997).

3 Hurvitz, pp. 280–281.

4 *Sutra of Forty-Two Sections*. (Burlingame, CA: Buddhist Text Translation Society, 1994, bilingual edition).

5 This chapter of the *Lotus Sutra* is also the origin of a practice common in the Buddhist tradition in China and Vietnam, when candidates for full monastic ordination, upon receiving the Pratimoksha, the 250 precepts of a monk or the 348 precepts for a nun, kneel and burn a number of spots—usually three or nine—on their head with moxa, a kind of herb that is also used in acupuncture. This ritual is an expression of their courage and their commitment to a life of practice and service in order to help living beings, and it is understood as a kind of offering to the Buddha, Dharma, and Sangha.

6 Hurvitz, p. 294.

7 Hurvitz, p. 296.

8 This and the following quotes are from Hurvitz, p. 316. Another version of these verses can be found in Thich Nhat Hanh, *Plum Village Chanting and Recitation Book* (Berkeley, CA: Parallax Press, 2000), pp. 291–294.

9 The *Heart Sutra* (*Prajñaparamita-hridaya-sutra*), presents the "heart" of the Prajñaparamita teachings on emptiness and nonduality. Written in the form of a discourse from Avalokiteshvara to the Buddha's disciple Shariputra, it is chanted daily in Buddhist monasteries and practice centers throughout Asia and in the West. See Thich Nhat Hanh's *The Heart of Understanding* (Berkeley, CA: Parallax Press, 1988).

10 An early Mahayana sutra that explicates the essentials of the meditative practice of the *shurangama* ("heroic advance") samadhi for the attainment of Buddhahood.

11 In Chapter 4, we first encountered the term "three realms" (*dhatus*).

12 Embracing Anger. Public Talk, 25 September 2001, Riverside Church in New York, NY.

13 In Vietnamese he is called Ong Ac. The kind man is called Ong Thien.

14 See Hurvitz, p. 316-318.

15 Hurvitz, p. 318.

16 Kshetra means land, region, or country.

17 "Heart of the Prajñaparamita," *Plum Village Chanting and Recitation Book*, pp. 15–16.

18   Thich Nhat Hanh. *Joyfully Together; The Art of Building A Harmonious Community*, (Berkeley, CA: Parallax Press, 2003).

19 Nom, is Vietnamese "vernacular script." After Vietnamese independence from China in 939 C.E., scholars began their creation of *nom*, an ideographic script that represents Vietnamese speech. For the next 1000 years—from the 10th century and into the 20th—much of Vietnamese literature, philosophy, history, law, medicine, religion, and government policy was written in nom.

20 Hurvitz, pp. 332–337.

21 *Plum Village Chanting and Recitation Book*, pp. 333–334.

Notes to Part Four

1 See also Chapter Twenty-Five, "The Six Paramitas," in *The Heart of the Buddha's Teaching*.

2 See Thich Nhat Hanh, *For a Future to Be Possible: Commentaries on the Five Wonderful Precepts* (Berkeley, CA: Parallax Press, 1993).

3 See *The Heart of the Buddha's Teaching*, p. 88.

4 For more on the Four Right Efforts, see *The Heart of the Buddha's Teaching*, pp. 92–93.

5 For an in-depth discussion of the teachings on consciousness, see Thich Nhat Hanh, *Transformation at the Base: Fifty Verses on the Nature of Consciousness* (Berkeley, CA: Parallax Press, 2001).

Index

PARALLAX
P
PRESS

Monastics and laypeople practice the art of mindful living in the tradition of Thich Nhat Hanh at retreat communities in France and the United States. Individuals, couples, and families are invited to join these communities for a Day of Mindfulness and longer practice periods. For information, please visit www.plumvillage.org or contact:

Plum Village
13 Martineau
33580 Dieulivol, France
info@plumvillage.org

Green Mountain Dharma Center
P.O. Box 182
Hartland Four Corners, VT 05049
mfmaster@vermontel.net
Tel (802) 436-1103

Deer Park Monastery
2499 Melru Lane
Escondido, CA 92026
deerpark@plumvillage.org
Tel: (760) 291-1003

For a worldwide directory of Sanghas practicing in the tradition of Thich Nhat Hanh, visit www.iamhome.org.